THE
JIMMY
HAGAN
STORY

THE
JIMMY HAGAN
STORY

ROGER BARNARD

The
History
Press

First published in 2007 by Stadia

Reprinted in 2010 by
The History Press
The Mill, Brimscombe Port,
Stroud, Gloucestershire, GL5 2QG
www.thehistorypress.co.uk

British Library Cataloguing in Publication Data.
A catalogue record for this book is available from the British Library.

ISBN 978 0 7524 4451 2

Typesetting and origination by Stadia.
Printed and bound in Great Britain

Contents

Introduction

As with many small boys, I was introduced to football by my dad and my team loyalties were settled for life from that moment on. The ground was Bramall Lane, the team Sheffield United and the date was October 1948. I was just approaching my ninth birthday.

My dad impressed on me that I wasn't just going to see Sheffield United but also to see the man who was a legend at Bramall Lane: Jimmy Hagan. 'He's the finest inside forward in the country and he should be playing for England,' I was told. I soon came to discover that this was the view of the majority of Unitedites.

Jimmy Hagan was the very heart of Sheffield United – the conductor, the orchestra leader and virtuoso soloist combined. His presence added thousands to the gate every time he appeared. He had amazing skill and ball control, a whole repertoire of tricks, he scored goals and could spray forty-yard passes unerringly to the feet of his teammates. His speed of thought was remarkable, sometimes too quick not just for the opposition but also his own team. He was the complete inside forward in an era which was blessed with a number of classic inside forwards.

Above all, Jimmy Hagan was an entertainer, and the fans loved to see him bamboozle defenders with some nifty footwork or a body swerve that would make seasoned opponents look ridiculous. It was all done with a deadpan face, for Hagan was not an outwardly emotional person and shunned any kind of personal glory. To some he appeared cold – a loner – but to his friends he was a warm and generous man with a dry sense of humour who could be the life and soul of a party, if he so desired. He could be stubborn, however, and always did what he believed to be right.

After a long career as a player with Sheffield United (1938-1958), Hagan became a manager, first with Peterborough United and then West Bromwich Albion. He was successful, but gained a reputation as a strong disciplinarian.

He was approached by the Portuguese club Benfica to become their coach in 1970 at a time when standards were slipping. Hagan soon knocked them into shape and Benfica went on to win three successive championships in his charge before he walked out on the club on a matter of principle. Apart from a spell in Kuwait, Hagan remained in Portugal where he was adored by the local fans, coaching and later living happily in retirement before returning to England for his final years. He died in Sheffield in 1998, just after his eightieth birthday.

It was typical of the man that he never wrote his autobiography, something he could easily have done if he had wished, for he was an intelligent and literate person. He would willingly discuss football in general, or his childhood in the north-east of England, but it was difficult to get him to even talk about his remarkable career. I hope this book will go some way towards filling the void, although he was such a deep and enigmatic character that even his own family had difficulty in understanding him at times.

This venture would not have been possible without considerable help from Jimmy's son, David, and daughter, Jackie, who assisted with the research and provided me with scrapbooks, cuttings and photographs, and introductions to a number of Jimmy's former colleagues and friends. I am also most grateful to Sheffield United FC for allowing me to delve into their archives.

Much has been written in the past about Jimmy Hagan (not all of it accurate), in the form of articles, obituaries and chapters in books, but I believe that we have unearthed some new material that will help to give further insight into a remarkable man and a bygone era of British football.

Roger Barnard
May 2007

Prologue

On 21 January 1998 a frail old man stood, with members of his family, admiring a selection of birthday cards laid out in honour of his eightieth birthday. The warmth of the messages was to be expected, but the remarkable thing was that many of the cards were from people he had never met. Alzheimer's disease had taken its insidious toll, but old memories were stirred and he seemed genuinely moved by the occasion.

One card, for instance, was addressed to 'Wonderful, wonderful Jimmy Hagan'. Another said: 'To my life-long hero, Jimmy'. A card with a large Sheffield United FC logo on the front contained the signatures of the then manager, Nigel Spackman and Tony Currie.

Hagan had returned to England to spend the autumn of his years, living quietly in Sheffield at Ascot Lodge, Gleadless since the death of his wife in 1996. Failing health had led him to leave Portugal in 1993, where he had lived happily for more than twenty years.

No fuss had been made of his eightieth birthday, outside his immediate family, and it was only when messages began to appear on the internet, saying that he was 'not very well', that football fans of all ages felt compelled to drop Jimmy a line.

The messages, which came from as far afield as Canada and the USA, were full of gratitude, admiration and affection: 'I shall always treasure the memories from your playing days with the Blades

– thank you!'; 'Get well soon from all the lads at Mount Pleasant FC'; 'From one blade to a great blade'; 'With admiration, with joy, and sincere regards'; 'I have always remembered your wizardry and brilliance – soccer heroes come and go but you have always been my only hero'; 'I never saw you play but you were a hero to my Dad – he has told me so many stories about you!'; 'Sheer artistry: Ringstead, Hagan, Browning, Brook, Hawksworth – I was brought up on that forward line. Thanks for millions of magic memories'; 'I was too young to ever see you play. It's said you were better than TC! You must have been one hell of a player!'.

A 'hell of a player' he certainly was: 'genius', 'maestro', 'Sir James', 'the Prince of the Lane', 'brilliant' were some of the epithets used regularly during his playing days with Sheffield United, but he was also a modest, private man, and something of an enigma, even to those who knew him well. His single full England cap was scant reward for a man who was regarded by many as one of the finest England inside forwards of his era.

He never 'sold himself' or went out of his way to make friends but he was hugely respected throughout the game – perhaps more than he himself ever realised.

CHAPTER ONE

Washington

Washington, County Durham, can claim that it was the birthplace of the ancestors of the first American president, George Washington. However, in the nineteenth and early twentieth centuries any fame had more to do with coal, for the town was situated on top of one of Britain's richest coalfields. Northumberland and Durham were dominated at that time by mining, and the whole area was pock-marked with numerous coal mines, coking plants, spoil heaps and all the muck and pollution that went with it. The area, the birthplace of the railway, was criss-crossed with railway lines and the main line between London and Edinburgh ran close by Washington.

It was an unhealthy place to live. Mining accidents were frequent. Men died, or were maimed, and those who avoided physical injury ran the risk of being blighted by silicosis, the dreaded lung disease caused by inhaling coal dust. The atmosphere above ground was hardly healthy either, smoky and polluted with soot and chemicals.

In the middle of this 'Hell's Kitchen' were the mining communities. People lived virtually on top of the pits in depressing rows of back-to-back terraced houses and miners walked to work, returning home still covered in coal dust. Wages were poor – bedding was often made out of sugar sacks for instance – but the community spirit was strong. Families stuck together, and neighbours helped each other out when times were particularly hard.

Despite all the hardships, people still managed to enjoy themselves. Football had become a favourite recreation towards the end of the nineteenth century and watching or playing in the local teams offered a release from the daily drudgery. In the narrow terraced streets, or on waste ground, small boys would spend hours kicking a ball around until called in by their mothers for mealtimes or bed.

Alfie Hagan was one such child. Born in 1894 from Irish immigrant stock on Pump Row, Waterloo, Washington, he attended the local school, erected by the colliery company, which could accommodate up to 600 children. Its main purpose was to provide a basic education and instil discipline and a sense of right and wrong in its pupils before, almost inevitably, the male children would head down the pit and the girls would be married off at a relatively young age. Alfie's ancestors came over from Ireland, probably in the latter half of the nineteenth century. The family name was actually O'Hagan but since there was prejudice against Irish immigrants which affected their job prospects the 'O' was quickly dropped and the name became 'Hagan' thereafter.

When Alfie left school in his early teens he followed the time-honoured route and went down High Usworth pit to work. There were few other options for a working-class boy except to work in the north-east's shipping industry. He was a strong, fit lad and played football for the colliery team.

Conditions at Usworth Colliery were no better, or worse, than many collieries at that time. The colliery worked three seams: the Maudlin, Low Main and Hutton. The sinking of the shaft had begun in 1845 and was finished in 1847, by which time it had reached some 1,000 feet below ground level. When Alfie worked at the pit it employed around 1,500 workers, of whom around 1,250 toiled underground.

Usworth had the dubious distinction of having suffered two mining disasters. On 5 January 1850 thirteen miners were killed in an underground explosion. On 2 March 1885 forty-two men lost their lives in another explosion when the deadly mixture of firedamp and coal dust ignited.

There were no more disasters after 1885 at Usworth, perhaps because safety measures improved, but people continued to die all too frequently in one-off accidents. The records show a variety of causes, from falls of stone to being crushed by machinery and, in one case, kicked by a pit pony. Tragically, the deceased were often mere boys – only in their teens. One Isaac Hagan, aged just thirteen, was killed at Usworth in 1898. Perhaps he was related to Alfie – the details have been lost in the mists of time – but he died apparently through his own foolishness. The record states, 'After ceasing work he was attempting to get on to a waggon which was being shunted into the colliery yard, when he fell under the wheels and received such injuries that he shortly after died.'

Alfie married Catherine Docherty, who happened to live next door on Pump Row and was fifteen on their wedding day. Catherine was the daughter of a ship's officer but she was orphaned at a young age and was brought up by her aunt and uncle. The newlyweds moved to another cottage owned by the mining company at Pear Tree Cottages, High Usworth. The house was rather better than many miners' families had to endure since it was one of a short row of four cottages adjoining some farm land. It had the typical outside toilet, coal house and prize leeks in the back garden. It also had the required loft to keep racing pigeons.

Alfie and Catherine would have nine children, one of whom died in early infancy. The surviving children were Nancy, Jimmy (born on 21 January 1918), Mollie, Alfreda, Sadie, Joyce, Dulcie, and Colin. Unfortunately, Alfreda died at the age of two after choking on food.

Their father was a strict disciplinarian with unpredictable moods and a hot temper. Any of his children who had, in his view, seriously misbehaved would be thrown out for a day or two. When the dust had settled, the kids would sneak back to the coal house and be fed by their mother who remained devoted and loving. It was said that Alfie would 'go off it' when he'd had his hair cut, or when there was a full moon – an exaggeration, no doubt, but by all accounts he was not a pleasant man, although he did mellow in his old age.

Alfie was a natural footballer and was playing for Usworth colliery at the age of fourteen. His progress in the game did not escape other clubs but the Football League and cup competitions were suspended after the end of the 1914/15 season so any thoughts that Alfie may have had about a football career had to be put on hold until the war ended.

He did enlist in the Army during the First World War but he was perhaps fortunate that his work down the mines took priority and he did not have to go overseas and become cannon-fodder. At the end of the war the nation's appetite for football was quickly restored and the League and cup competitions resumed.

Alfie was invited to play for Newcastle United as an inside forward in 1919. He scored on his debut (away at Manchester United) and played an integral part in the team until 1923, all the while working six shifts down the pit. Training and playing for Newcastle had to be fitted in around his mining duties. Apparently he was somewhat eccentric and there is a story that when he came up from a Saturday morning shift to go to St James Park to play against Tottenham Hotspur in 1920 he didn't have time to take a bath and had to play covered in coal dust. The fans weren't quite sure who he was! His journeys to Newcastle involved four miles by pony and trap to Heworth, from where he could take the tram into the city.

Newcastle United were remarkably consistent during this period, being in the top half of the First Division without ever threatening the very top teams. Their position see-sawed from eighth in 1919/20 to fourth in 1922/23.

In 1923 Alfie was transferred to Cardiff City who were a very successful team at the time. That season Cardiff were to lose the First Division title by the smallest ever margin on goal average to Huddersfield Town. Cardiff were also beaten 1-0 in the FA Cup final by Sheffield United in 1925. Alfie could not have dreamed that Sheffield United would become an important club for the Hagan family in the future, but he was on the receiving end of an 11-2 drubbing at Bramall Lane on 1 January 1926, which suggests a team rather the worse for wear after the New Year festivities, although Alfie himself did not smoke or drink. He finished his football career with Tranmere Rovers in 1929, just as his son, Jimmy, was beginning to show signs of a precocious talent in the game.

It was a tough life. The family remained in High Usworth while Alfie was away playing for Cardiff and Tranmere during the football season. Alfie sent money home and Catherine raised the family in the tradition of good Irish Catholics.

All the children attended the Catholic Elementary School, St Joseph's. This was typical of the schools of the day, with austere class-rooms and children sitting at wooden desks, in neat rows, all facing the front of the class where the teacher would stand by the black-board drilling home the 'three Rs'. Discipline was strict and the cane was often used, even for trivial misdemeanours.

The school was some distance from the Hagan home and all the children had to produce a chit on a Monday morning to confirm that they had attended church the previous day. When the younger sister, Mollie, managed to lose her chit, Jimmy pluckily stuck up for her, explaining to the priest that she was there along with the rest of the family in church the day before. The priest did not believe Jimmy and Mollie got the set punishment of a caning across her hand, at which point Jimmy, the oldest boy in the Hagan family, was so angry that he ran the three miles home to tell his father. Alfie was furious with the school, but pleased with his son who was already showing an unusual degree of initiative for one so young.

Shortly after this incident the school sent Mollie home ill. It was mid-winter and she had no one to accompany her. When the rest of the family came home, Mollie was nowhere to be seen and everyone was sent out to search for her. She was found unconscious in a ditch in the snow. When Alfie – who was in Cardiff at the time – heard about this he returned home, went down to the school and slapped the priest.

That was the last time the Hagan family crossed Catholicism. Alfie withdrew his whole family and placed them in the Church of England school just across the road from their house. Jimmy was delighted that he didn't have to walk three miles each way to and from school – and the fact that they had a better field for football was an added bonus.

Jimmy was excellent at his studies and was always near the top of his class. His father had given him a football when he was eight and he used to take it to school, keeping it under his desk so that he could play football in the playground at lunchtimes.

It soon dawned on the other children that they had a special talent in their midst. Eventually, he was allowed only one pick to play the rest of the class in unsupervised games. Jimmy nearly always chose the best goalkeeper, Wallace Fitzpatrick, and according to Wallace they would more often than not beat the rest of the class with Jimmy showing off his dribbling skills. It was at this stage that Jimmy used to go down to the colliery and watch the older lads playing on the flat colliery entrance area, and before long he was joining in.

With his father away so much of the time, Jimmy, the eldest son, grew up quickly. He helped his mother as much as he could and also kept an eye on the younger members of the family. When Alfie returned home, however, he expected Jimmy to toe the line and this led to clashes between the two: Alfie the strict disciplinarian, and Jimmy the stubborn, sometimes mischievous, youth who liked to have his own way.

Jimmy's excellent work in the classroom did not go unnoticed, and he was offered a place at the local grammar school. However, independent as ever, Jimmy turned it down because they did not play football. He was remarkably focused on the game and soon he was playing for the Usworth Colliery Intermediate School team at the age of twelve and also for Washington Boys.

Jimmy is reported to have played in 32 competitive matches during 1930 at the age of twelve, scoring more than 40 goals. The following year he scored 19 goals from his first eight games.

His passion for football did not prevent him from doing most of the things that other working-class boys of his age did, including keeping pigeons in the loft along with his father's prize birds.

He was naturally good at all ball games and in the summer months would play cricket where he proved to be a more-than-competent all-rounder.

To see the football stars of the day Jimmy would go along to Roker Park to watch Sunderland, or to St James' Park to see Newcastle United. Washington was well placed for this, being roughly an equal distance from both grounds. Both teams were in the First Division and always pulled in huge crowds. The north-east has always been a hotbed for football and Jimmy cannot fail to have been affected by the big-match atmosphere. One can imagine him returning home after a match, dreaming of the day when he might play on the big stage himself. Football then was primarily the working man's game and players, with their very modest wages, were regarded as working-class heroes.

The success of the young Hagan on the football field threw up the age-old problem of any sibling who follows in a sporting parent's footsteps. At heart, Alfie was surely proud to see Jimmy doing well, but it must have been painful to realise that his own football career had come to an end. What's more, there were strong indications that Jimmy would turn out to be a better player than he ever was.

The stern, unpredictable father and his talented and self-willed son clashed on many occasions. In one of Alfie's black moods he destroyed all the photographs and mementoes of Jimmy's fledgling football career. It was a bizarre thing to do and one can only guess at what was going on in Alfie's head at the time, although jealousy was probably the prime cause. Sadly, no decent photographs have survived of Jimmy as a schoolboy international – just a few faded newspaper cuttings.

On another occasion Alfie killed Jimmy's favourite racing pigeon. It may have ended up in the pot – as pigeons often did when food or money was scarce – but Alfie could be a thoroughly unpleasant – even violent – man, and was not averse to giving his wife a beating (something that Jimmy never forgot, or forgave his father for, for the rest of his life).

In one outburst, Jimmy was soundly thrashed when his father's prize leeks were pulled up in the back garden. Alfie accused Jimmy of doing this, wrongly as it happened, but when Jimmy revealed who the real culprit was he received another thrashing for not stopping him!

It is said that Alfie could have made enough money during his footballing career to be comfortably off, but he was an inveterate gambler and so remained poor for much of his life.

Jimmy must have been hurt and confused by his father's bizarre behaviour but he had already begun to develop a tough shell that would mask his true feelings and make him seem unusually mature for his age, setting the pattern for the rest of his life. The serious side of his personality was matched by an ability to have fun and enjoy himself, sometimes playing pranks that would get him into trouble. Certainly, as far as his football was concerned the problems with his father simply spurred him on.

By the time he was thirteen Jimmy was playing in schoolboy representative games at county level. Representing Durham in one closely-fought game against Yorkshire he scored the only goal but it was another player, Wilf Mannion, who attracted the most praise on that occasion. Neither Hagan nor Mannion could have realised that their paths would cross for the best part of the next twenty years, or that their respective skills – and the argument of who was the better player – would still be debated long after they were dead and buried.

It was almost a foregone conclusion that the young James Hagan was destined to go to the very top in the game and, in due course, he was selected to play in a schoolboys' international trial at Holiday Park in Durham. There was great excitement in the Hagan household when the letter arrived; Jimmy took it calmly – outwardly at least – but quietly made his plans to show off his skills. The diminutive Wilf Mannion was in the same trial at inside right and impressed with his clever footwork, but it was Hagan who scored, 'collecting a centre to shoot hard into the net', according to one press report.

Another report said: 'Hagan of Washington was a veritable artist with a ball. Indeed, he played so many tricks that at times he appeared to be slightly bewildered himself.'

Following his impressive display at Durham, Jimmy was chosen to play in another schoolboy trial at Chesterfield where he scored again with a left-footed drive.

Hagan did more than enough in these trials to be selected for a full schoolboys' international against Scotland at St James's Park in 1932, in which the young England team thrashed Scotland 5-0 in front of a crowd of 30,000 (such was the interest in schoolboy football at that time). Hagan relished the occasion, scored two goals and also hit the bar with another strike. A newspaper report of the match said: 'Chief among the winners' forwards were Lewis (the outside left) and Hagan. The former was fast and elusive and Hagan had clever control, dainty side touches, and a strong shot in his boots.'

One of the perks of playing for England at schoolboy level was that all the players received a cap. Jimmy, and the whole Hagan family, was immensely proud of the blue cap, with gold braid and a large tassel, that he brought home after the match. It was embroidered with the three lions of England and 'E v S 1932'.

Jimmy was also selected to play for England Schoolboys against Wales at Barry, during which the fourteen-year-old excelled and scored a hat-trick. One local newspaper said:

Jimmy Hagan, of Washington, was undoubtedly the 'star' performer, and even the keenest Welsh supporters were unstinting in their applause at some of his hard work. His ball control, passing, dribbling and shooting were outstanding.

Another report said:

Hagan, of Washington, at inside-left, was the schemer of the line. Rarely has a schoolboy given such a finished display in representative matches. His movements were much more quickly executed than in previous matches. Generally, his dribbling, placing and shooting were the great features of an interesting game.

This time Jimmy brought home a blue England cap, embroidered with 'E v W 1932'. Both schoolboy caps remained treasured possessions which Jimmy kept all his life. Now they belong to his family but are on loan to the Sheffield United 'Legends at the Lane' exhibition where they can be seen along with his other caps and medals.

Looking back, it is remarkable that both Newcastle United and Sunderland somehow failed to recognise the young Jimmy Hagan's talent. Had either of these clubs shown an interest it is likely that Hagan's profile would have been significantly higher.

Nevertheless, even before his stellar appearances in the schoolboy internationals a number of First Division teams had been alerted to his talents. By the time he was fourteen he was reported to be: 'an unusually well built boy of 5ft 4in and 8 ½st, and is developing rapidly. He is a born footballer and is captain of the county side this season. In addition he is an excellent cricketer and an all-round athlete.'

Just as today, football clubs were constantly on the lookout for promising youngsters and, although Football League rules forbade them from taking anyone on to their ground staff before they reached the age of fifteen, some poaching did take place, often with the promise of a job outside football as an added attraction. Several clubs were after the boy Hagan when he was just fourteen.

He was invited for trials by West Bromwich Albion, but it seems he did not impress them sufficiently to make a move. Bolton Wanderers, however, were keen to sign him, but could not find the lad a job. Liverpool then stepped in and signed Hagan, on amateur terms, from the club with whom he was registered, Washington Colliery. It is believed that Alfie had a hand in this (he still had many contacts within the game), but since Jimmy was not yet fifteen the Football League authorities intervened and forced Liverpool to release him. Interestingly enough, the Football League felt that Liverpool were paying Hagan too much for a youngster on the ground staff. The deal included £1 per week for his parents; the club paid for his digs and gave him a shilling or two in pocket money. The whole thing was deemed to be unethical, and Alfie missed out on his extra £1 per week!

A few months later, in May 1933 when Jimmy was fifteen, George Jobey, the manager of Derby County, signed Hagan legally and so began his development as a player in the Football League. The fact that Jobey had been a player in the same Newcastle United team as Alfie Hagan was probably no coincidence.

CHAPTER TWO

Derby County

Whilst Jimmy was well built for a schoolboy, he was regarded as rather too small and slim for the rigours of League football, playing against seasoned professionals twice his age. Derby concentrated on building up his physique and, much to the young James Hagan's frustration, he played very little football for the first few months, not even for Derby's third team. The lad lacked nothing in his mental approach, however: he was precocious, confident, and independent to the point of stubbornness.

When he first arrived at the club one of the Derby directors got him a day job as an apprentice motor mechanic, to give him a trade, but he quit after just a few days. Jobey found him back at the ground, training. 'What are you doing here, lad?' he asked. 'I didn't come here to work in a garage, Mr Jobey. I want to play football,' Hagan replied. Jobey was taken aback and angered by Hagan's attitude, and gave him an ultimatum: 'work or go home'. Without a word, Jimmy started to pack his bags. It was Jobey, who was regarded as a strong character, who climbed down and offered a compromise.

Jobey knew he had a rare talent on his hands. He told journalist Fred Walters:

I've got a lad at Derby who I think will make one of the greatest players of all time. He's only fifteen and I've never seen anything to touch him at his age. I'm only worried about one thing: he can be stubborn. He knows what he wants.

Jobey was not averse to blooding young talent in First Division football, however, saying: 'Let them have a taste of League football as early as possible, then they know at first hand what they have to achieve, and the rest is up to them.'

Hagan turned professional in January 1935 but he had to wait for nearly twelve months before he made his debut in the first team. There were, of course, no substitutes allowed in those days and a player had to last the full ninety minutes. In the meantime he played for the Derby Colts team, often receiving rave reviews in the local papers. In one 7-0 thrashing of West Bromwich Albion Colts, Hagan 'gave a brilliant exhibition, and was the outstanding player on the field'. He progressed to the reserve side, where he continued to impress: '…it had one star – young Jimmy Hagan. By far the best thing was his delightful skill and accuracy in working the ball. There was no forward on the field to equal Hagan in ball control and manoeuvres. The young Newcastle lad was a sheer delight.' But consistency at that age is difficult to maintain and he did have his off days, so even in the reserves his place was not guaranteed. It was a learning experience, but no different from that of any other young footballer. Hagan kept his head down, continued to work hard in training, watching and listening attentively to some of the older players around him.

Like so many other young players, Jimmy lived in digs, arranged by the club, and under the care of a landlady who would make sure that the lad behaved himself and did not get into any trouble. For the summer months Jimmy would return home to live with his parents, brothers and sisters.

During one of these summer holidays he acquired a whippet and, with some of his pals, decided to race it at South Shields. Unfortunately they had no transport and so walked the dog all the way from Washington to South Shields and back – a distance of about ten miles each way. Needless to say, it was too tired to make more than a token effort on the track!

His efforts at football were much more successful and in one reserve match against Newcastle United the local paper report was headed 'Hagan in Great Form'. The detailed account concluded:

> The star of the match was Jimmy Hagan. More alert than usual, faster on the ball, and showing remarkable ball manipulation on the difficult ground, Hagan introduced a stylishness that one rarely sees outside First Division football, and if he maintains this form he is certain to qualify for a place in the senior team.

He eventually broke through into the first team as a right-winger, as an emergency replacement for the England international Sam Crooks. The match was Derby County versus Everton on 28 December 1935 at the Baseball Ground. If Hagan was nervous, he did not show it. This was the fulfilment of his childhood dreams and he was determined to make the most of his chance. The final score was 3-3 and Jimmy provided the crosses for two of Derby's goals. He was twenty-four days short of his eighteenth birthday.

A newspaper report of the game said:

> Any review of the match must open with a tribute to Hagan, who at the age of 17, made his first appearance in League football – and made a pronounced success of it, too.
>
> Outside right is not the normal position of this gifted young player, but his natural aptitude for the game enabled him to make an excellent debut in nerve-testing circumstances. He showed confidence and craft in beating his man and he skilfully varied his services of passes from the wing.

Following the undoubted success of his first game at the top level, the young Hagan was now bursting to play regularly in the first team. Frustratingly, his chances remained few and far between since Derby had a strong, all-international forward line and Jobey was not going to drop his experienced players without good reason.

'Derby was a wonderful grooming place for a youngster,' Hagan said generously many years later. 'Who could fail to be inspired by such players as Hughie Gallagher, Jack Barker, Sammy Crooks, Dally Duncan, Charlie Napier and Jack Nicholas?' He added:

Mr Jobey was an amazing character. Winning on Saturday meant nothing to him. He still picked the team for the following game on how the players shaped up in the Tuesday morning practice match. I'm convinced some of those Tuesday games were the best seen at the Baseball Ground. Mr Jobey would stride up and down the touchline yelling at the top of his voice. You couldn't shirk a thing. County should have invited the public to pay for admission. The club would have made a fortune!

These early experiences of hard, competitive training sessions were to remain with Hagan for the rest of his career, sometimes bringing him into conflict with players when he was a manager.

He had to wait seven weeks for his next appearance, this time at inside right against Sheffield Wednesday, followed shortly afterwards by a match against Arsenal on 4 March.

Hagan ended the 1935/36 season with eight appearances and three goals. The first two goals both came in a match against Leeds United on 11 April 1936. Afterwards Jobey commented to the press: 'This eighteen-year-old lad is not exceedingly fast, but what nerve, coolness, skill, and confidence!'

He was beginning to be compared to Steve Bloomer, the legendary Derby County and England hero who played for the Rams between 1892 and 1912. One newspaper report claimed, 'the Crooks–Hagan wing is the finest since Bloomer's day,' and another said, 'there is not much sign yet of Bloomer's shooting power, but he has the great English amateur's knack of making wonderful moves in an easy way – the mark of a master player.'

Despite success on the field, and growing popularity with the Derby fans, Hagan had a difficult relationship with the manager, who found him 'idiosyncratic'. Perhaps Jobey felt that he never had the young Hagan fully under his control; although Jimmy had shown himself to be a hard worker and quietly efficient as a scheming inside forward on the pitch, away from it he was a bundle of good-humoured mischief.

During his time at Derby County Jimmy met a girl who won his heart – Iris Baxendale. Iris worked as a secretary for Rolls Royce in Derby and the two were introduced by the then Derby County winger Alf Jeffries who, coincidentally, joined Sheffield United in 1939. From their first meeting they became, in modern parlance, an item, and the couple saw each other regularly.

Jimmy continued to find his chances in Derby's first team limited by the high quality of their other, more experienced forwards, but his talents had not been missed by other teams. One of these was Sheffield United who in 1938 were pushing for promotion from the Second Division. They saw in Hagan a player who could provide a little extra up front and in November 1938, with 30 League appearances and 7 goals under his belt, Jimmy was sold by George Jobey to the 'Blades'.

The transfer fee was £2,925 – a substantial sum in those days. Teddy Davison, the Sheffield United manager, refused to pay Derby's asking fee of £3,000, perhaps on principle, although Hagan was still relatively unproven at the senior level. By now Hagan weighed around ten stone. His wages were the standard £7 per week, to be topped up by a £1 bonus when he was picked for the First team. He received the maximum signing-on fee of £10.

CHAPTER THREE

Sheffield United

Jimmy Hagan arrived at Bramall Lane as a slim, dark-haired, good-looking twenty-year-old with a growing reputation as an intelligent and very talented youngster with exceptional ball control, good balance and a strong shot with either foot. Whilst he was tipped to become a great player, he was not yet the finished article, though his transfer caused plenty of favourable comment among the Sheffield United fans.

In the Sheffield United dressing room, where many players had 'seen it all before', his arrival did not create any undue excitement. Hagan was a quiet young man, and not one to push himself forward. Sheffield United had some good, experienced players, and some promising youngsters of their own. Although they had been in the Second Division since 1934 they had reached the cup final in 1936 and had twice narrowly missed out on promotion. At the start of the 1938 season the club had bought Harold Hampson from Southport for £2,200. Now Teddy Davison was banking on Hampson and Hagan to supply the extra quality to get the team back into the First Division.

With no television to showcase the talents of rising stars, reputations were made largely by word of mouth or from reports in the national and local newspapers.

The use of substitutes was still many decades in the future so new players could not be eased into a team by giving them a run out for the last few minutes of a match. It was all or nothing in those days and Hagan was thrown in at the deep end for his first match in the red and white stripes of the Blades on 5 November 1938, when he immediately established himself in the side. He was given the no. 10 shirt and thus started in the inside left position in an away game against Swansea Town. The team won 2–1, with the goals coming from the burly centre forward Jock Dodds and left-winger George Jones.

The following week Hagan played in his first home game against Chesterfield, again at inside left. The team drew 1–1.

It was perhaps felt at this point that Hagan's relatively slim build was something of a handicap for an inside forward, for he was switched to right wing where he formed a partnership with Hampson at inside right. Hagan's first match on the wing, against Tranmere Rovers, saw the team win 2-0, with both goals coming from Jock Dodds. Then, on 26 November, Hagan scored his first Sheffield United goal in a 3-1 win over West Ham United in front of the home crowd of nearly 20,000. He scored in the next game, too. The quiet young man was letting his feet do the talking and, in a small way, the legend of Jimmy Hagan had begun!

In February 1939 Davison strengthened the team still further with the £5,500 purchase of Bobby Reid, a Scottish international left-winger from Brentford, but Jock Dodds was sold to Blackpool for £10,000 and was replaced by George Henson, a £2,600 buy from Bradford. In the reshuffle, Hagan was moved to inside forward. Apart from a couple of games missed through injury, the versatile Hagan was to play regularly until the end of the season – a total of 33 matches shared between inside left, inside right, and outside right positions.

He was steadily adding to his goals tally, too. Coming into the last game of the season against Tottenham Hotspur he had scored eight. The final game on 6 May was critical: Blackburn Rovers and Sheffield Wednesday had completed their fixtures and were already established in first and second positions in the Second Division.

United could do nothing about Blackburn, who had already secured promotion, but a win over Spurs would see the Blades leapfrog into second place over the Owls, and thus gain promotion at the expense of their Sheffield neighbours and arch-rivals.

In front of a crowd of 38,460 at Bramall Lane the team turned on the style. Hampson scored after just ten seconds, Hagan added three fine goals and Henson chipped in with a couple in an emphatic 6-1 victory. Hagan's performance in the match was little short of sensational and his goals were all splendidly executed, perhaps the best being when he dummied the Spurs keeper to send him the wrong way before scoring. Three years later the Spurs wing half who had tried to mark Hagan during the match was heard to remark: 'That bloody Hagan – I'm still dizzy!'

Fans celebrated the Blades' success at getting back into the First Division, but all the talk was of Jimmy Hagan, the twenty-one-year-old football genius who had become the star of the team. Hagan took it all in his stride and remained outwardly unaffected by all the accolades coming his way. He was still the quiet, thoughtful, polite young man with the maturity of a much older player. Perhaps, as Colin Collindridge said many years later, 'he was ten years before his time'.

Years later, the *Independent* journalist Ivan Ponting wrote: 'At Bramall Lane he blossomed, his fluent distribution, magnetic control and shrewd positional play inspired the Blades.'

When United kicked off the new season in the First Division on 26 August 1939 against Liverpool, Hagan opened his goal account with one in a 2-1 victory. But the war clouds were already gathering and thoughts were turning away from football towards the likelihood of conflict. War was declared on 3 September 1939 and after just three matches, in which United were unbeaten (with two wins and a draw), the Football League programme was abandoned. Many footballers' contracts were cancelled and they found themselves out of work. They had few options: enlist with one of the national services, do essential war work in one of the 'reserved occupations', or wait for the inevitable call-up.

With memories of the slaughter of the First World War still relatively fresh, for all young men of fighting age it was a time of great uncertainty and worry. For Jimmy Hagan, a twenty-one-year-old with the football world seemingly at his feet, it must have been immensely disappointing.

CHAPTER FOUR

Aldershot

After a short break, friendly matches were organised, and then a regional league was set up, but Sheffield United's successful promotion team was breaking up fast. Some players were called up into the armed forces, whilst others remained closer to home with 'reserved civilian employment' in essential services, such as the mining or steel industries, or munitions work, and so were able to play regularly. A system of guest players was established so that teams could utilise anyone who was available, although Sheffield United, in fact, did not make much use of this system.

Hagan continued to play in the friendly matches and the new Regional League East Midlands Division until he was called up in December 1939. Leave during Christmas and Easter allowed him to play in a handful of further matches and, in all, he made 24 appearances during the 1939/40 season, all in the inside left position, and he scored nine goals (including a hat-trick against Rotherham United).

Jimmy was enlisted into the Army Physical Training Corps at Aldershot where he qualified as a PT instructor. He was determined to make the best of his situation and he knuckled down to his military duties, which fortunately allowed him time to play football regularly. During the remaining war years his appearances for Sheffield United were very limited, amounting to just a handful of games per season, but he was invited to guest for Aldershot FC, for whom he would play 92 games between 1940 and 1944 and score 45 goals.

The year 1940 also saw Jimmy marry his fiancée, Iris Baxendale, and the wedding took place in Derby, where Iris still lived. The war played havoc with family life, of course, and whilst Jimmy was in the Army Iris continued to live with her parents until he was demobbed after the war.

Aldershot had one of the largest Army training camps in the country and, because of this, Aldershot FC, with its guest players, was able to turn out a very strong team during the war, sometimes with a complete XI made up of guest players. In addition to Hagan, other guests included internationals such as Tommy Lawton, Frank Swift, Cliff Britton, Stan Cullis, Denis Compton, Joe Mercer and Wilf Copping, all of whom were serving in the Army.

Tommy Lawton wrote in 1946:

> In the small number of games I was able to manage for the Southern club the hard-wearing Lawton boots cracked in ten goals. Some of these scores were due to the assistance I got from Jimmy Hagan, the Sheffield United inside forward. Jimmy and I worked up a grand understanding, which stood us in good stead when we played for England together.

Aldershot were managed by Bill McCracken, a former international who was reputedly the inventor of offside tactics.

The PT Corps deliberately targeted professional footballers to train as instructors because of their fitness levels and familiarity with training routines. Whether strings were pulled or not, many of the big-name footballers remained in the UK, where they were available for representative games between the services, and also the morale-boosting wartime international matches. Compared to many of their military colleagues serving overseas, they had a relatively cushy life. However, all of them were trained soldiers and had to be prepared to fight for their country if necessary. Jimmy remained at Aldershot until 1944, although in some respects he was lucky to survive the war at all.

At some time between 1940 and 1944 (the exact date is unknown) Jimmy fell ill with pneumonia. Antibiotics that would be used routinely today were not available then, and when he failed to respond to treatment he was admitted to Cobham Hospital, seriously ill. For a critical few hours it looked as though he would not pull through, and a priest was called to give Jimmy the last rites. A surgeon operated to drain fluid from one of his lungs, and slowly he began to respond. The crisis over, he recovered rapidly, the only evidence of his brush with death being a permanent scar on his back, caused by the operation. His excellent physical condition must have been a factor in his recovery, for he was soon back on duty – and playing football again.

Hagan started as a sergeant but he rose to the rank of WO Class II (company sergeant major instructor). Many details of his war service are sketchy but when he was based at Aldershot he would have been knocking the new recruits into shape, improving their fitness through PT activities and games.

Elsewhere, every battalion had a PT Instructor who was responsible for the physical fitness of about 800 men, keeping them in readiness for battle. They looked after all the sports equipment and organised the PT sessions – and also recreational activities, too. It is generally accepted that the corps was well trained and motivated, and did a first-class job. Jimmy Hagan took his role very seriously and pictures of him during this period appear to show a man who was proud to be doing his duty. In his later years he often spoke fondly of his time in the Army. He enjoyed the camaraderie with his colleagues and, of course, he was able to play his beloved football regularly.

Physical fitness was regarded as essential by all the armed forces, and that included a wide range of sports and games. The Army Sport Control Board published a weighty manual of nearly 600 pages (*Games and Sports in the Army*) to outline its principles and explain the rules and background to a wide range of sports, with particular emphasis on football, athletics and boxing. The PT instructors would often be called upon to organise sports and games for the troops, and they would be expected to understand the rules and procedures of the more popular games, and act as referee if necessary. Jimmy took all this in his stride since he was a natural sportsman and an excellent cricketer, as well as a footballer.

The Army Physical Training Corps issued fitness charts as a guide for all Army personnel, showing exercises to be done on each day of the week (except Sundays). These charts were illustrated by the cartoonist Fougasse and the sets of pictures bore slogans such as 'Flat Foot is Fatal to Fitness', 'Inactive Internals Indicate Inefficiency', 'Never Neglect the Neck', 'Easy Waist Exercises Eliminate Exhaustion', 'Shoulders & Spine Should be Supple & Strong' and 'Sixty Seconds Sport Skipping Strengthens Stamina'. Hagan absorbed the messages behind these little slogans, which encouraged him to maintain his own physical fitness throughout much of his life.

The war provided a huge disruption to many professional footballers' careers but Hagan's war service did give him greater physical strength and body weight. There is also the strong probability that playing with many seasoned internationals for Aldershot FC actually accelerated his career as an international footballer.

Whilst he was in the Army there were many representative football matches that went unrecorded, but the Hagan scrapbook contains a photo of him in an Army side that played Ireland in 1941, with the words 'Three goal Hagan! Good Luck' written on it by a well-wisher.

Another (undated) press cutting shows Hagan, with Denis Compton, Leslie Compton, Stan Cullis and Cliff Britton, all in Army uniform, breakfasting in the Caledonian Hotel before playing an Aberdeen Select XI at Pittodrie.

Yet another photograph, marked 'Ireland 1943', shows a relaxed Army team in uniform, posing for a photograph outside a railway station. The commentator and journalist Raymond Glendenning has sneaked into the picture at one end, and Denis Compton is pictured with cigarette in hand – a sign that smoking was then more accept-able for sportsmen than it is today!

Raymond Glendenning, with his trademark handlebar moustache and thick-rimmed spectacles, often travelled with the England team to wartime international matches and so became well known to Hagan and the other players.

It did not take long for Hagan to become an England international. Whilst his Aldershot and Army connections may have accelerated his progress, his star quality would surely have been recognised sooner, rather than later, had the war not intervened. Nevertheless, England was truly blessed with skilful forwards at the time and Hagan had to compete with the likes of 'golden boy' Wilf Mannion, Raich Carter, Len Shackleton, and others.

Since the country was at war, the international games were local affairs between England, Scotland and Wales. The FA deemed these to be 'unofficial' internationals, which is unfortunate for those who took part in them since the players did not receive caps or medals – just a certificate.

Hagan was nevertheless immensely proud to be chosen for his first international – an England versus Wales match, played at the City Ground, Nottingham, on 16 April 1941, when he was twenty-three years of age. The game was watched by just over 13,000 people and England won 4-1.

This was just the start of an international career that saw Hagan play regularly for England for the next three years, becoming not only an established part of the team but also a regular goalscorer.

In a match against Scotland at Wembley on 17 January 1942 Hagan certainly made his mark by scoring after just fifty seconds. Taking a pass from Mannion, and catching the Scotland defence unprepared on the icy surface, he wriggled his way through to score with an unstoppable shot.

The following week Hagan was in action again as part of a strong Army side against the Belgian Army at Aldershot. Life was certainly not all square bashing for the wartime footballers!

Just a few weeks later the Army played a strong Football Association XI at Aldershot. Tommy Lawton remembers it as:

> Definitely Jimmy Hagan's match. The sprightly little inside forward with the very dry sense of humour rammed in a couple of snap shots in the first half and we ran out 3-1 winners. Jimmy is one of the most dangerous inside men I have played with, and only those close to him on the field realise just how brilliant he can be.

In those days international footballers really did play for the honour of representing their country, for there was precious little financial reward. They often had to make their own way to the ground, meeting up for the first time in the changing room on the day of the match, or in a hotel the evening before the game, and they would enter the ground unheralded by the players' entrance. Although rail travel would be paid for, the match fee was not even paid in hard cash, but players were given two fifteen shillings National Savings certificates. Practice sessions were a luxury that could not be afforded in wartime, but the players were all professionals and were expected to know what to do. England did not even have a manager at that time, just a selection committee.

Early in 1943 Hagan played in a match against Wales at Wembley which pulled in the largest wartime crowd to date and was also attended by the King and Queen, who were presented to the players. Hagan – the twenty-five-year-old son of a coal miner – was almost bursting with pride when he shook the sovereign's hand that day. England went on to beat Wales 5-3 in a scintillating game in which the whole England forward line (Matthews, Carter, Westcott, Hagan and Compton) was in sparkling form. Hagan did not score, but gave what was described as 'a constructive and unselfish display' and had a hand in at least three England goals.

Following this match Hagan was part of a strong English Army FA side against a Scottish Army team at Hampden Park. The English Army won 7-0, with Jacky Robinson of Sheffield Wednesday scoring four and Westcott the other three. A newspaper report at the time said: 'It was Robinson and his great Sheffield rival, Jimmy Hagan, who bewildered the Scottish defence and at times had them watching helplessly.' An unusual feature of this match was that the Scottish side was allowed to field a substitute in the second half to replace an injured player – the first time this had been allowed in an Army International game.

Hagan also played in the next proper international, against Scotland at Hampden Park on 17 April 1943 in front of 105,000 fans – most of them rooting for the home team. In a 4-0 win, Raich Carter scored two of England's goals, the others coming from Westcott and Denis Compton, whose brother, Leslie, won his first England cap as a defender. The Compton brothers were remarkable in that both were fine cricketers, too: Denis as an England batsman of the highest quality and Leslie as a wicketkeeper who could also score runs on his day. Both played county cricket for Middlesex for a number of years after the war. Denis Compton had first met Hagan when playing in an international schoolboy trial and, although in the Army, served in the Royal Engineers, and not in the PT Corps. Compton was to play in ten wartime internationals, and would probably have played in more had he not been posted to India.

Three weeks after the Scotland game Wales and England fought out a 1–1 draw at Ninian Park, Cardiff. Wales scored first with a 'soft' goal and then held England at bay. The Welsh full-back, Lambert, had the measure of the England left-winger, Denis Compton, throughout the match until eight minutes from the end when Compton and Hagan switched places. Jimmy promptly beat Lambert for the first time in the match and sent over a perfect centre for the Wolves' centre forward, Westcott, to score from twenty yards.

On 25 September England played Wales at Wembley. The 80,000 crowd certainly got their money's worth since England won 8-3. The match was by no means one-sided for, although England led 4-1 at half-time, Wales pulled it back to 4-3 before England forged ahead again with Hagan breaking both the offside trap and the Welsh spirit to score the fifth goal. Hagan scored twice in this match, but it was one of the few occasions that his wife, Iris, was not in the stands to watch Jimmy play. She was in a London hospital, recovering from an operation, and Jimmy had taken time out to visit her before setting off for Wembley. The match also saw the first substitute allowed at Wembley. A Welsh player (Ivor Powell) broke his collarbone and the England management offered the England twelfth man, Stan Mortensen, to take his place. Mortensen, who had not yet played for England at that time, was the best 'Welshman' on the field and contributed to his team's revival early in the second half.

Wales had been scheming all week on how to stop Stanley Matthews, and instructed both their left-back and left half to watch Stan closely throughout the game. The plan backfired for it gave more room for the other forwards, which Carter, Welsh and Hagan gratefully exploited.

England were definitely on top form at this period for at the next international on 16 October 1943 they scored another eight goals to beat Scotland 8-0. Sixty thousand fans squeezed into Maine Road, Manchester for this memorable game. Hagan again scored two of the goals. Tommy Lawton wrote in his book, *My Twenty Years of Soccer*, 'I can honestly say that I have never played in a better side than the England one that day.'

Frank Butler wrote after this match:

The big surprise of the war is that during this world conflict England has produced its best Football team of all time... I put it down to the fact that England had 11 Servicemen (seven Army/four RAF). These men are fitter today than four years ago. More strenuous training and stricter discipline has improved their physical fitness and their mental alertness for a 90-minute test.

Add to this the fact that the players have got together in unit and representative matches, and now know each other's moves by heart. The Carter–Matthews right wing turns out in RAF matches. The Hagan–Compton wing represents the Army. The Britton–Cullis–Mercer half-back line is naturally the Army's choice. Scott and Hardwick are RAF backs.

There is also fine comradeship among the team. Denis Compton, Hagan, Cullis, Britton and Hardwick travelled in a party to Manchester. They passed the journey playing solo-whist and wise-cracking at the expense of their captain, Stan Cullis, who is a far better footballer than he is a solo player!

Now take Scotland. The team consisted of four Servicemen. The rest were from factories, shipyards and mines.

The success continued on 19 February 1944 when England played Scotland again at Wembley. This time the score was 6-2 to England and Hagan scored his now-customary two goals. It is surprising to note that Hagan, after being almost a regular in the England side for nearly three years, and scoring many goals, had still been regarded in some quarters as not worthy of an England place. After the Scottish game, however, there could be few doubts. L. V. Manning wrote:

HAGAN HITS THE HEADLINES.

One of the interesting points for England was the bold stepping out of the modest Hagan, who up to now has been a little overawed by Carter and, quite understandably, hasn't found Compton easy to play with.

I wrote last week… that if Carter played close to Matthews at Wembley Hagan would star in bigger type on the England bill.

That's how it worked out. For the first time since they came into the team we saw Carter and Hagan working together with the perfect understanding of Hall and Goulden of beloved memory.

On 15 April 1944 Sheffield United played a wartime cup semi-final at Villa Park and Hagan managed to obtain leave from the Army to play for his club side (for only the second time that season). The manager, Teddy Davison, could not go to Birmingham because of the illness of his wife but since the railway system was in a chaotic state he asked the Sheffield journalist Fred Walters to meet Hagan at the station and take him by taxi to Villa Park. Walters secured a taxi, with some difficulty, and met the train from Aldershot, but Hagan wasn't on it. Walters got the taxi to drive from Exchange Street to New Street to meet another train – still no Hagan. The next hour saw the taxi driving back and forth between the two stations – until finally Hagan arrived with his football boots in a parcel under his arm. The problems were still not over, however. There was such a crowd outside Villa Park (44,000 watched the game) that the taxi could not get through. Jimmy had to sprint the last quarter-mile and just made it in time to play.

Despite all the pre-match drama, Hagan scored one of the Blades' two goals, but unfortunately Villa scored three. The cup was a two-legged affair and the teams met again a week later at Bramall Lane (unfortunately without Hagan who was required on international duty) but could only draw, so Villa went through to the final, leaving United pipped at the post.

A journalist at the time commented:

Sheffield United might have been in the Cup Final North instead of Aston Villa, if their soldier inside-left, James Hagan had been able to play in the second leg of their duel. But this player was wanted on international duty. Incidentally, he has become an almost automatic choice for the England side: one of the big war-time 'finds'. This fellow Hagan seems likely to go down on the list of one of the game's curiosities: to be included among the men who get to the top and stay there without any flare of trumpets. There's nothing flashy about him; nothing particularly clever or outstanding unless you watch very closely, but just an honest-to-goodness and all-round efficient trier who puts the side first, second and third, which means that the solid work he does often goes unnoticed.

Whilst United and Villa were battling it out at Bramall Lane, Hagan was playing for England against Scotland at Hampden Park in front of 133,000 fans. England managed to survive in this hotbed of

Scottish fervour to win 3-2. England's goals came from Lawton (2) and Carter.

This was the last wartime international that Jimmy was destined to play in, for after this match he was posted to France along with thousands of other British troops who were now on the offensive in Europe. Attached to the Royal Wiltshire Infantry, he went across to Normandy on D-Day plus six.

In the Wales versus England game on 6 May 1944 Hagan's inside left position was filled by Johnny Rowley of Manchester United.

His departure from the international scene certainly did not go unnoticed, however, as one newspaper report pointed out: 'Chief problem is adequately to replace Cullis and Hagan. The selectors may have to acknowledge the impossibility of finding players comparable with these two.'

Hagan's job at this stage in the war was to keep the troops active and interested when they were pulled out of the front line for a rest. He greatly admired the work done by the infantrymen and made some good friends amongst them – friendships that would last for decades.

Jimmy and his colleagues even managed to play football at this time, whilst war was raging not far away. If there was a football pitch nearby they would try to organise a game, although sometimes they had to fill in the bomb-holes before they could kick off!

CHAPTER FIVE

Germany

Even after the war was won in Europe, troops did not return immediately to the UK since there was still soldiering to be done in the devastated German cities and, in any case, it was impossible to demobilise all the troops at once. Jimmy Hagan's unit was posted to Hamburg. There was now no need to maintain the troops in battle fitness, but to keep them occupied and happy the emphasis turned more towards games. The PT Corps ran courses to instruct soldiers on the basic rules of all games, partly to prevent boredom, but also to give instruction to those who wished to take up a teaching or coaching role after they were demobbed

Hagan's wartime duties never put him in the firing line. He later joked that the only time he ever raised a gun in anger was when he was arranging a football match between regiments. After rowing across a river to inspect the pitch he found the locals had removed the crossbars for firewood. Hagan drew his gun and ordered them to put the crossbars back in time for the match. His bluff succeeded and the match went ahead on schedule.

Hagan was never one to show much emotion, but one incident in Germany did affect him deeply. He was part of the British Army contingent that liberated the notorious Bergen-Belsen camp on 15 April 1945. The inmates had been abandoned by the Germans and left to die. The British found 10,000 unburied corpses and 40,000 sick and dying prisoners. Among the 40,000 living inmates, 28,000 were in such a bad state that they died after the liberation. Hagan seldom spoke about the experience, but he did confide to his family many years later: 'It was terrible – the worst thing I've ever seen in my life.'

Jimmy managed to earn some home leave in September 1945 and was able to turn out for Sheffield United in the derby match against Sheffield Wednesday on 8 September at Bramall Lane. This was his first appearance for the Blades since the cup semi-final on 15 April 1944 and although more than 30,000 watched the match Hagan must have wondered if the trip over from Germany had been worth it, for the Blades lost 1–3.

Around this time British soldiers in Germany found themselves with time on their hands and some enterprising officers in the 53rd (Welsh) Division near Dusseldorf realised that they had a number of former professional footballers amongst their ranks.

The footballers were put in the charge of Sergeant Major George Swindin, the Arsenal goalkeeper, and began to train together. Although fraternisation with the former enemy was officially forbidden, the Army team ignored this and began playing German teams who approached them for fixtures. The games attracted many enthusiastic supporters, both British and German.

Jimmy Hagan happened to be in the Dusseldorf transit camp, en route to Hamburg after some home leave, when the local Army team had arranged to play a match with Schalke 04, the German champions. This was the Army team's toughest test so far, and since defeat would have resulted in serious loss of prestige, Hagan was asked if he could bolster the side. Never one to turn down the chance of a game of football, Jimmy happily agreed, and the necessary permission from his superiors was obtained to stay on in Dusseldorf. It was a brutal game in which one British player suffered a broken leg, but British pride was maintained when the Army won 2–1. Apparently several players wanted to be captain for that match, but reports suggest that Bill Shankly was given the honour, owing to his seniority.

It is well known that the war changed many people's lives. Years spent serving in the armed forces, learning new skills, experiencing life-changing events and forming lasting friendships left many people determined to make a fresh start when they returned to 'civvy street'. Jimmy Hagan, it seems, was no exception.

Frank Yates, a Sheffield man, who many years later would become chairman of the Senior Blades, was then a young officer with the 53rd Division and recalls that, sitting with Jimmy in the restaurant overlooking the Wuppertal Stadium before the Schalke match, he told him that he couldn't wait to see him back at 'the Lane'. To his dismay, Hagan replied that he was unlikely to return to Sheffield United. He complained that there was little money in football and no prospects for the future. He said he was thinking of taking up a different career with better long-term prospects.

Perhaps this was just a temporary bout of pessimism – not untypical of Hagan – for one would have thought that, as a current England international with a job awaiting him at Sheffield United when he left the Army, Jimmy would have been looking forward to resuming his career. However, he was by nature a cautious man who often agonised about things and took nothing for granted. Happily, the moment of despondency soon passed and he never raised the subject again.

Sheffield-born Sergeant Major Peter Cooper was in charge of the Wuppertal stadium which the RAF had fortunately left intact during their many bombing raids. As a member of the PT Corps and a regular soldier who had joined before the war, he was senior to Jimmy and he ran physical training courses at the stadium. Peter and Jimmy had met a few times over the years at refresher training courses. Whilst he was present for the Schalke match Jimmy eyed the excellent facilities at the Wuppertal stadium, which included a cycle track, a fine gymnasium, and even a restaurant, and he asked Peter to do him a favour. Jimmy said he had only a few months to go before he was demobbed and persuaded Peter to apply to get him transferred to Wuppertal from Hamburg (where conditions were more primitive).

This was done and the pair became room-mates for about four months over the winter of 1945/46 until Jimmy returned to Britain to be demobbed. Like Frank Yates years later, Peter Cooper became a member of the Senior Blades, although since he remained in the Army until the late 1950s he never saw Jimmy play for Sheffield United. The two kept in touch over the years, however, and remained friends.

Peter remembers Jimmy as someone who was easy to get on with, but who was socially not very outgoing. During this post-war period a number of games were arranged with visiting rugby or football teams (one of which was Arsenal). After these there would usually be a party when the players and officials would let their hair down, sometimes with a selection of local frauleins invited as dancing partners. Jimmy, however, who did not drink, would tend to sit quietly to one side and not get involved. Nevertheless, he seemed to enjoy the occasions in his own way.

Hagan's conversations with Peter invariably centred on football, which seemed to be the main focus of his life at this time. Any earlier misgivings about his future that he had discussed with Frank Yates seem to have been resolved, for the time being at least.

He was less forthcoming about his personal life, however, and Peter cannot recall Jimmy saying much about his family back home in England. When Hagan was not holding PT classes or arranging games he could often be found in the gymnasium alone with a football, practicing his ball control. Peter remembers going to the gym to watch him, with admiration bordering on awe, as he went through his repertoire of tricks.

Throughout the war, Jimmy's taciturn nature did not go down well with some of his colleagues who resented the fact that he was not more outgoing. He was not a shy man but was undoubtedly a bit of a loner, though certainly never arrogant. His work as a PT instructor was exemplary, as was everything he set his mind to. He could be impatient with others, and did not suffer fools gladly, but his dry sense of humour was never far below the surface, and this could lead him to be mischievous with colleagues and friends. He enjoyed a game of cards, but just did not feel the need to be sociable for the sake of it, and was rarely 'one of the lads'.

Hagan was selected again for the England side against Wales on 20 October 1945. The side had struggled in its previous match against Ireland and several newspapers rejoiced at the return of its former automatic selection at inside left. One headline proclaimed 'Hagan should put rhythm back in England attack'; another, 'Hagan's return is England asset'. Transport was organised so that Hagan could be flown from Germany to take part in the match at The Hawthorns, West Bromwich Albion's ground. However, Hagan was carrying an injury, perhaps a legacy of the battle against Schalke, and the day before the game he had to pull out. The twelfth man, Malcolm Barrass, took his place in the side.

As Jimmy looked forward to returning home for good, there were the first signs that the old order in football was changing. In November 1945 a strong Russian team – Moscow Dynamo – visited Britain and played several matches. It soon became clear that the Russians were the equal of the best British League sides. They played attractive football at a terrific pace with rapid and accurate inter-passing with the ball being pushed along the ground. Wonderful ball control and exceptional fitness were the key and it was very much a team effort. Dynamo went back to Moscow unbeaten, having given the British football establishment some food for thought. Hagan was not involved in any of the matches against the Russian side, but it is certain that he would have taken note.

Hagan's football undoubtedly reached new heights during the wartime years and he was one of England's greatest successes at international level during the period.

CHAPTER SIX

Demobbed

Jimmy returned to England in February 1946 and was delighted to be back with his wife and family again, although Britain was virtually bankrupt after the war. Strict rationing of food and clothes was the order of the day and virtually everything was in short supply. After six years away there were some inevitable readjustments to be made as he prepared for civilian life and he insisted on taking a couple of weeks to get himself match fit and mentally ready before returning to football.

He was officially released to Class 'Z' Royal Army Reserve on 29 April 1946, and would remain on the reserve list until June 1959, although he was never required to serve in the Army again. The Hagan family moved into a flat on Southbourne Road, near the Botanical Gardens in Sheffield's leafy Broomhill district. He was able to play in eleven games for Sheffield United up to the end of the season, wearing the no. 10 shirt.

Hagan's inclusion in the side had not been a foregone conclusion since the team was enjoying a good run and there were some fans who did not want to see the successful side disrupted. The management thought otherwise, however, and Hagan was immediately (and controversially) made captain. He was quick to prove his worth and scored five goals, in addition to his all-round contribution to the side.

Henry Rose wrote in the *Daily Express* around the middle of March:

> Full marks to the Sheffield United Club management for not heeding the clamour of some of their followers to keep intact a winning team. The clamour meant the exclusion of recently demobbed English international Jimmy Hagan. It reached its height when the United brought off a dramatic 2-1 win at Blackpool on February 23.
>
> Jimmy was there – as a spectator. For two games he looked on and then said he was fit. He was immediately made captain in the face of criticism and the decision has been amply justified.
>
> Hagan has been the inspiration of the League leaders' last three victories. His display at Anfield against Liverpool was streamlined – a delight to the eye, everything done with a minimum of effort and the maximum of effect.
>
> No wonder his attractive young wife was almost bursting with pride.

Rose also wrote, in a separate article:

> I discovered the secret of the breakneck speed of all the Sheffield United eleven. This is it. They assemble for training only once a week; they are too far apart for more than one all-get-together.
>
> When they strip, contrary to long-accepted Soccer practice, they put their football boots on – not pumps, spikes, soft shoes or the like. They do this whether there's a ball about or not. Sprinting, lapping, all are done with boots on. The answer is 28 league points out of the last 30. Full marks again to manager Ted Davison and trainer-coach Duggie Livingstone, a man who has always been full of ideas.

With Hagan back in the side and playing superbly, the 1945/46 season saw Sheffield United win the League North Championship, putting them and their supporters in good heart for the resumption of proper League football the following season.

In the midst of this Hagan was selected to play in an international trial match at Wembley. The game was an Army XI versus an FA XI. Hagan's front-line colleagues were Denis Compton, Tommy Lawton, Don Welsh and George Wardle. Denis Compton wrote in his book *Playing for England*: 'A special word, I feel, is due to the unselfishness of both Jimmy Hagan and Tommy Lawton. Some of the passes they sent out to me were of the copy-book variety; no player could but help do moderately well with such service.'

This match led to both Compton and Hagan being selected for England in the forthcoming Victory International against Scotland at Hampden Park on 13 April 1946. Somehow 139,468 spectators squeezed into the ground, to see the home team beat England 1-0 with a goal scored in the last thirty seconds. Scotland were on top throughout and it is likely that the decision of the Scottish FA to call the players together a couple of days before the match – instead of meeting for the first time in the changing room before the game – paid dividends.

Denis Compton, back in action after Army service wrote: 'Personally, to have Jimmy Hagan by my side again, was wonderful. It seemed, when we began to find each other with the ball, that my months abroad had been nothing more than a dream.'

Unfortunately these post-war 'Victory Internationals' still did not qualify players for a full England cap.

Hagan was next picked for the England versus France game on 19 May at the Colombes Stadium in Paris. France won 2-1 but Hagan did score England's goal. The team was a blend of the old and new, with a line-up of: Williams (Wolves), Bacuzzi (Fulham), Hardwick (Middlesbrough), Wright (Wolves), Franklin (Stoke), Johnson (Charlton), Matthews (Stoke), Carter (Derby), Lawton (Chelsea), Hagan (Sheffield United) and L. Smith (Aston Villa).

In all, Jimmy played in 16 'unofficial' Wartime and Victory Internationals, scoring 12 goals (possibly more, since some records are incomplete).

Jimmy and Iris had much to be pleased about on 19 July 1946 when their first child, David, was born. With the new football season still around six weeks away, Jimmy had plenty of time to learn about the joys of fatherhood and bond with the new member of the family.

Despite (or perhaps because of) the harsh restrictions of post-war Britain, the 1946/47 season was greeted with great expectation by a nation starved of top-class professional football. Nowhere was this optimism more marked than at Bramall Lane. The old ground had suffered major bomb damage during the Sheffield blitz in December 1940 when ten or eleven bombs fell on it, destroying a large part of the John Street stand and the roof of the Kop. There had also been at least two bomb craters on the pitch itself at the Bramall Lane end. The ground had been closed for the rest of that season (the remaining home fixtures being played at Hillsborough), but it had been patched up in time for the 1941/42 season, though still bearing many of its scars that would remain until well after the war.

CHAPTER SEVEN

First Division Football Again

The team took its place in the First Division and, as players gradually returned from war service to augment those who had remained in Britain, the Blades were able to turn out a well-balanced and competitive side. Unlike Hagan, many had played regularly for the club throughout the war years, thanks to having jobs in the mines, steel mills or local military bases. Among these, Harold Brook, Colin Collindridge, Albert Cox, Fred Furniss, Ernest Jackson, George Jones, Albert Nightingale, Harry Latham, Stan Machent, Walter Rickett, Jack Smith and Denis Thompson were still available. A bonus was Alex Forbes, who had struggled to shine as a forward, but proved to be a revelation at wing half.

Jimmy Hagan, however, threw a large spanner in the works when he told the club management that he would not sign a new full-time professional contract. He was still concerned about his future, and that of his wife and young son, and felt that he should have a qualification to fall back on when his playing days were over. He was only twenty-eight and, as things turned out, had another twelve years' top-level football in him, but he was not to know that. As always, on a matter of principle, he dug his heels in. To try to persuade him to sign, the club bought a house for Hagan (at a time when property was scarce) but, independent as always, he refused it (although he did accept a club house a few years later). Meanwhile he was happy enough in his flat on Southbourne Road.

A national newspaper summed up Hagan's dilemma:

Rumour is busy concerning the future of one of our best forwards in football – James Hagan of Sheffield United. He hasn't re-signed for that club: apparently wants to go elsewhere, and is even said to have dropped hints of going out of the game altogether. The one certainty is that football can't afford to lose him. He's too good.

It is worth noting that in the late 1940s the life of a professional footballer, despite its moments of glamour and excitement, was a precarious one. The better players earned a reasonably good wage for the time (compared to the average working man) but there was always the risk that a serious injury or loss of form could see their career curtailed at a relatively young age, with precious little in the way of compensation. For married footballers, with children, it was a constant worry for their wives. Iris Hagan told a Sunday newspaper journalist in 1949 that she hoped her son would never become a professional footballer, and if she ever had a daughter, she hoped she would never marry one!

Jimmy joined a local firm of architects (George Morton and Colin Rayleigh) to train as a surveyor and he failed to turn out for the Blades in their first five games. Then Sheffield United gave in and the club agreed to his demands. A deal was struck for him to play on a part-time basis.

Part-time players were by no means uncommon at the time (another Blades' favourite, Jack Pickering, had played under such terms). Even so, most first-teamers were on full-time contracts and perhaps the club had felt that Hagan was not fully committed to the team. However, Jimmy was such an important player that he could dictate his own terms to some extent. These terms did not affect his earnings, since Football League clubs still had to adhere to a fixed maximum wage structure that was hardly generous and did little to reward the most talented players. Jimmy Hagan may have been a part-timer in name, but he certainly gave his all on the pitch and his fitness was never called into question.

His surveying studies meant that he could not train regularly with the first-team squad, but instead he trained on Tuesday and Thursday evenings with other part-time players. He also reported on Wednesday nights for additional training and every morning got up at 6.30a.m. so that he could do a five-mile run before setting off for the office. Thanks to his Army PT training his weight had risen to nearly eleven stone, giving him strength on the ball to add to his box of tricks.

'I felt I had to keep really fit,' he said later. 'Sitting in an office all day was something quite new to me.'

As things turned out, Hagan's football career went from strength to strength and he quit working as a surveyor after a few years and never gained the professional qualification that once had seemed so important to him.

There is some mystery about the exact terms of Jimmy's part-time contract, for there is no record of his wages in the Sheffield United archives in the late 1940s. Just how he was paid, and by whom, remains a puzzle.

Hagan also had the ability and good sense to dabble in journalism. He had experience at the highest level and many good contacts in both the game and the media, and he developed this extra string to his bow. He had a bylined article in a Sheffield newspaper as early as October 1946, and this was to expand into a regular weekly column by 1953.

The 1946/47 season started with mixed fortunes, Sheffield United achieving just one win and three draws from their first five games. After Hagan's reintroduction the side managed a couple of victories and went on to win 13 more games up to the second week in February.

Then the notoriously bad winter of 1947 arrived with a vengeance and games had to be postponed or quite often played under dreadful, frozen conditions which would not be tolerated today. United's form dipped alarmingly and the team lost six out of the next seven games. A late rally came, along with the thaw, and because of all the postponed games, the season dragged on into the middle of June.

Nevertheless, the team had an excellent FA Cup run, reaching the sixth round before being eliminated by Newcastle United. The fifth round saw them fashion a late 1-0 away victory at Stoke City on a frozen desert of a pitch that, according to the journalist Peter Wilson:

> …had only a purely coincidental connection with any football pitch I have ever seen. Remember the icy conditions were entirely against a player with the nimble-footed craft and the deft touches of Hagan. Yet after the match a director of another club said to me in the board room: 'That was the greatest display of leadership I've ever seen on the football field.' And he went on to suggest that without Hagan Sheffield United would be rather like a rice pudding if you left out the rice.

Desmond Hackett, writing about the same match, said: 'It was Hagan who made the goal that left Stoke a beaten team, bewildered that such a thing could happen in the last minutes of a game which had been nearly all the Stoke way.'

It was perhaps during this season that Jimmy Hagan really became the idol of Bramall Lane, where to most fans he could do no wrong. Certainly, since his arrival in 1938 he had put in some dazzling individual performances, and he had been almost a regular in the England side, but because of the war the Bramall Lane faithful had seen only fleeting glimpses of Hagan's skill.

Now the 'part-timer' Hagan, who was still captain, was receiving accolades virtually every week from the press. When United played Arsenal at Highbury in November, one newspaper report said:

> Outstanding in the visiting attack was Hagan, who by his distribution of the ball, tactics and all-round leadership, kept the men together in attack and defence.
>
> It was due to the leader's persistence that his side opened the scoring when Compton, in passing back, beat his own keeper.

It seems that Hagan had learned a thing or two about Denis Compton during all the Army and England games they had played together!

Just a week later United beat Blackpool 4-2, giving their best display of the season to date on a very muddy pitch. Hagan scored a brilliant goal after just three minutes when he strolled through the mud-bound Blackpool defence, had his shot blocked by the keeper, and followed up the rebound. After this the Blades never looked back and they used the heavy mud to their advantage. One journalist wrote: 'Hagan was in brilliant form, his footwork at times being almost uncanny, and he was easily the most polished footballer on the field.'

The frantic Christmas and New Year period was largely fruit-ful. United thrashed Brentford 6-2 at Bramall Lane on Christmas morning, with Hagan scoring two; the Boxing Day return match at Brentford saw United lose 1-2, but this was followed just two days later with an away win against the high-flying Liverpool (who won the First Division title that season). United won 2-1 with goals from Forbes (penalty) and Nightingale and the away team increasingly dominated the proceedings as the game wore on.

The journalist Sydney Gibbon wrote:

This lively Sheffield side, led by one of Soccer's masters, in Hagan, has a Cup look about it. There is a high level of teamwork, even though both goals at Anfield are traceable to the genius of Hagan and his readiness to do anything and everything. He was full-back, centre forward, corner kick taker rolled into one with an ease that made it look child's play.

Fred Walters, the *Green 'Un* writer, was fulsome in his praise:

Hagan, leading his white-shirted colleagues, was the presiding genius in a feast of very fine football, and if there is a finer inside forward playing today, I am Emperor of China… United's halves were a superb line, and gave a courageous and highly skilled display, with Hagan frequently dropping back as a sort of liaison officer between forwards and halves.

It was a strategy which paid handsomely. Hagan was the individualist of the game, without a doubt – a very great player of today.

Another journalist, writing of the same match, said:

Shining star of the 22 players was Hagan. What a player! The ball was always his servant. His touches charmed the 50,961 crowd (thousands were left outside) and flummoxed the defence.

Hagan was everywhere, now helping the defence, now starting an attack, and even taking corners. His play was, I hope, an object lesson to the inmates of the boys' pen. Hagan is captain of this United side, and a great one too.

One week later, on 4 January, United beat Leeds United, at home, 6-2 on a glue pot of a pitch, with Hagan scoring one of the goals. R.A. Sparling wrote in the *Sheffield Telegraph*:

No team is faster, no team is blessed with greater stamina, and no team is more adaptable than Sheffield United. And the team spirit is excellent.

The genius in the side, of course, is Hagan, who ranks with the cleverest inside forwards the club has ever had. There is a threat behind every pass he makes and his brain is ever plotting.

Fred Walters wrote:

In the first half in particular Hagan was positively brilliant, and I dare say that Leeds, like many other teams this season, must have wished he had been on their side instead of against them. It was a very hard game on an appalling ground.

…Hagan was again in one of his brilliant moods – one of those days when it is difficult to think there is any forward in the game to approach within any distance.

Of Hagan's goal:'There were no half measures about the way he fired the ball past Twomey.The goalkeeper, literally speaking, never saw it.'

A commentary in one of the local papers summed it up:

> People up and down the country are beginning to sit up and take notice of Jimmy Hagan again. On his present form he cannot be left out of England teams in spite of the success of Carter and Mannion in earlier internationals.
>
> What one likes about Hagan is the fact that he can serve up a worthwhile game no matter what the conditions – whether the ground be dry, heavy, or frozen. Few can do this.
>
> About 12 months ago misguided United fans were saying United would make a mistake to disturb their winning team to find a place for Hagan... by now they must realise the club possesses one of the most consistent as well as brilliant forwards.

Hagan produced many fine performances that season but none more so than on 29 January 1947 when United beat Wolves 2-0 in the FA Cup fourth-round replay. Hagan was at his dazzling best and outwitted the formidable half-back line of Galley, Wright and Cullis. Wolves were one of the top sides in the country at the time and missed being the First Division champions by a single point.

For the final game of the season United faced Stoke City at Bramall Lane. Had they won, Stoke would have taken the League title, and it has been alleged that before the game certain Stoke players, who were apprehensive of United's robust style, took some United players to one side and suggested they could earn a few extra quid by throwing the game.The Sheffield players would have none of it and United beat Stoke 2-1, consigning them to fourth place. Hagan was in no way involved with any of this chicanery for he was injured and did not play in the match. In any case, he was a stickler for doing the right thing and, had he played, would never have countenanced throwing a game. United secured sixth spot in the First Division, which was very respectable, but could have been so much better had the side been more consistent. Whilst United played lively attacking football, the defence conceded too many goals. The team had a reputation for being strong in the tackle, nevertheless.

At the end of the season United had scored 140 goals from their 42 matches, more than the League champions, Liverpool, who scored 126. These were the days of all-out attack and high-scoring games: Wolves scored 164, Manchester United 156 and Stoke City 142 for the season. No wonder that coaches began to concentrate more on defence in the coming years!

Hagan was captain for much of the season, quietly leading by example rather than throwing his weight around, either on the field or in the dressing room. As for tactics, Teddy Davison was of the old school of secretary-managers and was hardly seen in the dressing room. Team tactics were left to the trainer-coach, Duggie Livingstone, but once on the field it was up to Jimmy to organise things. One former player says the only tactics he can recall were to give the ball to Jimmy and let him weave his magic. Over the years coaches and managers learned that they could instruct the team on how they wanted them to play, and Hagan would nod his head in apparent agreement, but then he would go out on the field and do things his way. Reg Freeman (United's manager from 1952 to 1955) said, 'At team talks he agrees politely and then ignores it all on Saturday.' Hagan knew, better than anyone, how to get the best out of the other players and was generally regarded as the best United captain since the legendary Billy Gillespie.

Ernest Jackson, the accomplished wing half for the Blades until 1949, and trainer from 1952 to 1955, once said: 'He's very difficult to understand but he'd always be the first name on my team sheet.'

For this, and several seasons that followed, the Bramall Lane pitch was in a poor state, not helped by the wartime bomb damage. By November most of the grass would have worn off, apart from a little near the corner flags, and very often the ground would be a mud bath. There was one particular spot at the Bramall Lane end where a bomb crater had been filled in, and this could get particularly sticky.

Above: 3. Derby County FC 1936/37. The eighteen-year-old Hagan is on the second row, second from left.

Right: 4. Looking somewhat older than his twenty-one years, Jimmy as a Sheffield United player in 1939.

Opposite above: 5. The Army had a strong football team during the war, with many international players. Jimmy is on the front row, second from right, next to Denis Compton (with cigarette).

Opposite below: 6. A proud moment for Jimmy was to be introduced to King George VI before the England versus Scotland international at Wembley on 19 February 1944. The players include, from left to right: Tommy Lawton, Joe Mercer, Hagan, Stanley Matthews, Leslie Smith.

7. Jimmy scores for England against Scotland at Wembley in 1944 – England won 6-2.

8. Hagan captains an Army team in Germany in 1945.

11. Hagan was not noted for his heading ability, but he nodded this one in against Everton in 1949, only for it to be ruled offside. War damage is still visible at Bramall Lane. (*Sheffield Telegraph & Star*)

12. Hagan battles for the ball against Cookhill of Notts County, October 1950.

15. The victorious Football Association Canadian tour squad arrives back in Liverpool, 1950.

16. Hagan strikes for goal against Nottingham Forest in United's promotion season, 1952/53. (*Sheffield Telegraph & Star*)

19. Hagan with Joe Mercer after the latter's arrival as manager in 1955. Jimmy wore his England blazer on this occasion – perhaps to give his old friend a gentle reminder? (*Sheffield Telegraph & Star*)

20. In the manager's hot seat at Peter

21. Jimmy, Iris, Davi
and Jackie at home i
the early 1960s.

24. Although over fifty, Hagan led the gruelling training sessions by example.

25. Torres
of Benfica
practices
the long
throw und
Jimmy's
watchful

Above: 28. When Jimmy took over as coach of Sporting Lisbon he introduced the same unorthodox methods as he had done at Benfica to improve fitness levels.

Below: 29. Jimmy had the players running up and down the terraces to improve fitness. They hated this and some were physically sick at first.

32. Jimmy was feted by play
fans after the cup win. The
lucky mascot.

33. After Jimmy's death, Sh
United commissioned a bro
to commemorate their grea
player.

Hagan and Collindridge sometimes worked a routine to take advantage of this and wrong-foot defenders who were not familiar with the terrain. As an attack built up Collindridge would station himself in an area which would force the covering full-back to stand in the 'bomb hole'. Hagan would then slip the ball inside the full-back for Collindridge to run on to, leaving the full-back literally bogged down!

In the 1946/47 season Hagan played in 33 League and five FA Cup games for United, scoring 15 goals. Only Collindridge scored more, with 18, and it was clear that this left wing partnership was a potent force for Sheffield United. Harold Brook, the inside right, also scored 15.

Hagan played a couple of representative games for the Football League against the Irish League during the 1946/47 season: on 19 February 1947 at Liverpool, winning 4-2, and on 30 April 1947, in Dublin when the Football League won 3-1 and Hagan scored.

Fans of Hagan's era will remember him as a seemingly unemotional man on the pitch, whose face wore a deadpan expression irrespective of how well or badly the game was going. Even his scoring a goal would hardly raise a smile. As he trotted back to the centre circle the only celebration would be a brief handshake with one or two of his colleagues. Nevertheless, this calm exterior was misleading: Hagan firmly believed that it was a footballer's job to entertain the spectators and score goals, and he certainly put his views into practice.

Beneath the surface the poker-faced Hagan was a complex character. Outwardly quiet and reserved, he was nevertheless good company with his friends but he would never sell himself to win favours or seek to influence people. Only once can his former team-mates remember him losing his rag, and that was during a practice match when he came to blows with the United wing half (and former marine) Harry Hitchen. The incident was soon over, however, and nobody can remember what caused it, although Hitchen was a strong, physical player and it is possible he caught Hagan with an over-enthusiastic tackle.

Despite his success as a player, and all the praise that it brought from fans, the media, and indeed fellow professionals, Hagan remained very much with his feet on the ground and disliked any kind of adulation. He did not have a strong bond with many of the players, although if he did take a liking to someone the friendship tended to be sincere and long-lasting (conversely, there were a few others that he took an instant dislike to and nothing would make him change his opinion). As one of his friends commented many years later, 'It seemed almost as if Jimmy deliberately chose his friends. Even then you could never get really close to him.'

Off the field there were some players that he hardly spoke to, although almost all respected him. If he did have something to say he did not mince his words and usually said what was on his mind. There were times when players did get together after a match, or when they were in a hotel for an away match, and on these occasions Hagan could be sociable and he genuinely enjoyed such times. He had a fund of card tricks and other party games that he had picked up in the Army, and he would happily entertain (and sometimes baffle) the others with these. He also had a dry sense of humour, was an excellent mimic, and was not averse to practical jokes. On one occasion a few of the players had been chatting up a group of attractive women who were staying at the same hotel. One of the players who had fancied his chances heard a knock on his bedroom door at 11.15p.m., and thought his luck was in, only to be confronted by Jimmy who was wearing a party mask!

He would stand for no nonsense, however. Colin Collindridge remembers one occasion after the war when the team was staying in a hotel in London prior to an away match. An Irish waiter accidentally knocked over a vase of flowers and some of the water spilled into Hagan's soup. The hapless waiter's response was to pour the surplus water off the top of the thick vegetable soup into another flower vase and hand Hagan back his soup bowl. Hagan gave the waiter a long, withering look and said 'Take this away!' This was one of the very rare occasions that any of the players saw Hagan come close to losing his temper.

There is no doubt that Hagan was on a different wavelength from many of his colleagues. He enjoyed music, and would go to orchestral concerts at Sheffield's City Hall. Sometimes, after training, he would go down to Willson Peck's music shop in the centre of Sheffield, usually accompanied by the United winger George Hutchinson, who was also a classical music buff. Willson Peck's had booths where one could try out gramophone records, and Hagan and Hutchinson would request a number of records from the counter, then retire to a booth where they would play the records and discuss the relative merits of tenors, Caruso, Gigli, etc.

He enjoyed the musical variety theatre, too, and would often visit, with Iris, the Empire or Lyceum theatres in Sheffield. The comedians Jimmy Jewell and Ben Warris were pals of Hagan's and would send him a couple of tickets whenever they were performing in town. The comedians were big Blades fans, so Jimmy was able to reciprocate with tickets for the occasional United home game.

Jimmy liked parties, too. He did not drink alcohol, of course, but he could be the life and soul of the occasion. He had a liking for fancy-dress parties, where he and Iris would turn up in some outrageous costumes.

This aspect of his personality is at odds with the picture which was sometimes painted of a somewhat withdrawn person whose close friends were relatively few. He was certainly an enigma.

CHAPTER EIGHT

Mixed Fortunes

Teddy Davison (who had been Sheffield United's secretary-manager since 1932) had succeeded in building up a successful football team by prudent buys and the development of local talent, but he now seemed to lose his way. He set about dismantling the squad, selling some established players, and replacing them with others of dubious quality. No doubt the board backed this policy for they seemed willing to sell any player – irrespective of his value to the side – if they received an attractive offer for him. Hagan remained as captain and the focal point of the team for the 1947/48 season, until he was sidelined from the beginning of January until the end of March through injury.

As far as the fans were concerned, football was booming, perhaps as a relief from the drab austerity that was a feature of post-war Britain. Crowds for home matches seldom dropped below 30,000, and the highest of the season (against Derby County) was 51,893. It was a season of mixed fortunes and United struggled to a mid-table finish in twelfth place. Hagan played 29 League matches and scored six goals.

He also played for the Football League against the Irish League in Belfast on 22 October 1947, scoring a goal in a 4-3 victory.

It was clear that Hagan was still the brightest star in a rather lacklustre Sheffield United. After they beat Preston North End on 20 September 1947, R.A. Sparling was drawn to write:

If I had to choose a world's best XI from all the star players I have seen during the last quarter of a century, I should include Jimmy Hagan… Today Hagan has as much ball magic and art as Matthews. Several times on Saturday he had three or four men round him. Occasionally they paused as though spell-bound, and frequently he wriggled his way through the lot. The secret of it is hard work. Hagan devotes several hours each week to practising with a ball.

This last sentence may seem surprising today, but training in the 1940s often consisted of fitness work without a ball. Many coaches felt that if players were starved of the ball during the week, they would be more likely to use it well when Saturday came around.

By now Hagan, aged twenty-nine, was at the peak of his career. Good looking, dark-haired, 5ft 9ins tall and weighing about 11st, he was equally at home on the left or right, and could turn up almost anywhere on the pitch to make a telling contribution to his side. He was never regarded as a fast player but was quick enough to beat most defenders. His football brain was super-fast – too much for opponents, and sometimes for his own side as well. His ball control was perfect, seldom needing a second touch, and he had the ability to collect a high ball and instantly wheel away in one sweet movement as though, as Joe Mercer later put it, 'he had a claw in his boot'. He was two-footed and could shoot with both power and accuracy. He had a trick for seemingly every situation and was very difficult to tackle or dispossess. He played in an era of tricky inside forwards but there were very few who could match his prodigious skill and ball control then – and there have been very few since.

His method of trapping the ball was superior to that of most players since it gave opponents little chance of intercepting it. He would receive the ball whilst standing still, appearing merely to flick his foot upwards at the ball as it neared the ground and then, as though it was part of his foot, the ball came down under his toe without any force, and remained there as though fixed with glue. As soon as the ball reached the ground Jimmy was ready with both feet to move off at any angle. It all appeared so simple, yet few other players could do it with such apparent ease.

He was rewarded with an England 'B' cap against Switzerland 'B' in the summer of 1948, details of which seem to have been lost in the mists of time.

In later life, Hagan said that the player he most admired was Peter Doherty. Here was another gifted, intelligent inside forward who believed in creative, constructive and attacking football, although he was a more mercurial character than Hagan, a brilliant dribbler with the ball, but also a worker and fighter who never stopped running. Hagan, by contrast, often appeared to stroll through the game. You would seldom see him chasing lost causes; he expected the ball to be passed to his feet, after which he would take control and build another attack.

Raich Carter, himself another great inside forward, wrote in 1949:

> During my associations with Sunderland, Derby County, the Royal Air Force and England, I have played with many inside forwards. Of these, three names come into my mind as the most outstanding, Peter Doherty, Jimmy Hagan and Wilf Mannion. To play alongside such good players was a sheer delight.

Whilst Hagan's own standards did not diminish, the 1948/49 season was a poor one for the weakened team, which finished at the bottom of the First Division. Hagan played 44 games that season, in both the inside left and inside right positions, and scored 13 goals.

The bright spot for Jimmy was selection for his first full international match, on 26 September 1948 when England played Denmark in Copenhagen. At last Hagan had an England cap to take home!

The Danes were amateurs who, two months earlier, had finished third in the Olympics and this was their first ever match against professional opponents. The England team was Swift, Scott, Aston, Wright, Franklin, Cockburn, Matthews, Hagan, Lawton, Shackleton and Langton with John Aston, Jimmy Hagan and Len Shackleton making their full international debuts. It looked a strong line-up on paper but, in fact, the match ended in a 0-0 draw. England's forwards were unable to make an impact against a packed Danish defence on a heavy, rain-soaked pitch and the England team was criticised for their shot-shy performance. It marked the end of Tommy Lawton's England career after 22 games and 23 goals, not counting his 25 goals in wartime internationals.

It may have been Hagan's first full international but there is no doubt that he was among friends. When in Denmark he played a trick on Frank Swift who was happy to relate the tale some years later:

I first got to know Jimmy well in the Army team during the war, where he earned the reputation of a practical joker. But I never learned how good a mimic he was until the England visit to Copenhagen.

Tommy Lawton and I, who shared a room, were continually being pestered by phone calls from a 'Danish newspaperman' offering us a fabulous amount of cash for any exclusive stories about the England team – at a time when the FA had forbidden us to open our mouths to the press.

The mysterious voice in pidgin English strung us along for four days, and even at the airport as we were leaving, there was another phone call for 'Meester Swift'.

This time I was almost talked into giving a 'scoop' when I suddenly caught sight of Jimmy Hagan holding the phone in an adjacent booth – with Stan Matthews, Stan Mortensen, and a gang of England players beside him laughing their bloomin' heads off. I felt about three feet high!

Hagan and Swift remained good pals. Once, in a League game in which Frank Swift was the opposition's goalkeeper, Hagan had been on the receiving end of some brutal treatment and had spent the latter part of the match hobbling painfully on the wing. There were no substitutions in those days so an injured player had to stay on the pitch if he possibly could. At the end of the match the trainer came on to assist Hagan off the field, but big Frank strode up, brushed the trainer aside, picked Hagan up bodily and carried him off, to the applause of the spectators.

Frank Swift was a big, genial character who could always raise a laugh, sometimes unintentionally, such as the time when he arrived for an away League match with two right boots. He had such large feet that he was unable to find a left boot to fit him at short notice and had to play the match wearing two right boots. He could pick up the heavy leather ball with one hand and throw it to the halfway line with ease. Among his accomplishments was once serving as a lifeboatman at Blackpool. His regard for Hagan was clear when he described him as 'the best football artist in the British Isles'.

The Denmark game proved to be Hagan's only full international, although for several years there was a persistent clamour for him to be included in the England side – and not just from the Sheffield fans and press.

Sheffield United historian Denis Clarebrough wrote:

He belonged to an era when international footballers did not expect to be told how to play the game, or what time they should go to bed. It was Hagan's misfortune that his first post-war cap coincided with the appearance on the scene of Walter Winterbottom, England's first soccer manager. Hagan, Tommy Lawton and three or four others disappeared from the international scene and it was some time – and only after enormous public pressure – before Stanley Matthews wore an England shirt again.

It has been suggested that Winterbottom felt that Hagan – for all his individual talent – could have threatened his authority since Jimmy had a reputation for doing things his own way and would certainly not have been intimidated by the England national coach. However, there is no evidence that this was so and, in any case, Winterbottom's brief was purely team preparation and tactics. Team selection remained in the hands of a selection committee.

In fact, Hagan was an admirer of Winterbottom's methods and never spoke critically of him. Walter Winterbottom, the FA's director of coaching, first took charge of the England side in 1946 and led them to a 7-2 victory over Northern Ireland. No subsequent England manager has ever presided over such a resounding victory on his first game in charge.

Tommy Lawton always said that he had the highest regard for Hagan's talents. Once, after scoring six goals in a game for Aldershot, he put it down as 'a personal triumph for Jimmy Hagan'.

For the 1949/50 domestic season in the Second Division Harry Latham took over from Hagan as team captain – a move which was not universally popular with the players. Some reports say that Hagan resigned the captaincy; others that the move was forced on him. Whatever the truth of the matter, his attitude remained exemplary and he continued to play his usual game as the focal point of the team.

At the end of September 1949 Hagan was actually dropped from the first team for four games. Things were clearly not running smoothly behind the scenes, for these were the last days for trainer-coach Dugald Livingstone who had been with Sheffield United since 1936. Livingstone left the club on 14 October and the reserve-team trainer, Reg Wright, took over. Hagan was immediately restored to the first team.

The season saw United make a valiant effort to get out of the Second Division, but in the end they were just beaten into third place by Sheffield Wednesday by the narrowest of margins.

Spurs, who had some fine players, won the League by a nine-point margin, and were a class apart that year. A dreadful 7-0 thrashing at White Hart Lane in November certainly damaged United's chances. Hagan had a lengthy spell out injured from the end of January until mid-April, but the reshuffled forward line managed pretty well without him and the team was in second place by the end of February.

Hagan returned just in time to score a brilliant late winning goal against Spurs at Bramall Lane on 15 April (had Ted Ditchburn, the Spurs' goalie, not pulled off two brilliant saves Hagan would have had a hat-trick) and the team won their last three League matches – the final one against Hull City by a 5-0 margin. It was not quite enough, however. Sheffield Wednesday still had one more match to play – against Spurs at Hillsborough. A defeat would give promotion to United. A 1-1 draw would result in a tie for second place, but a 0-0 draw would be sufficient to see them through by a marginally better goal average. United's supporters were unimpressed when the two teams played out a goalless draw, although mutterings by some that the game must have been fixed were probably unfounded. Spurs hit the post during the match but, with nothing to play for, probably already had their minds on the following season.

Hagan played a total of 29 games in all competitions that season and scored seven goals. His goals-per-game ratio had dropped a little over the past couple of seasons but this probably was the result of his playing a deeper role – more like a modern central midfield player – and supplying the ammunition for the other strikers.

Hagan's late season return to action after injury ensured that he could take up an invitation to join the Football Association's tour of North America. The FA party sailed from Liverpool en route to Quebec on the *Empress of Scotland* on 9 May 1950 with eighteen players, two officials and a trainer. The party included Stanley Matthews and Nat Lofthouse, and several other players of note but, curiously, only one goalkeeper.

The two month-long tour saw the squad play ten games across Canada, although there is no record of how many Hagan played in, or the results. Football in Canada could not compete with ice hockey and baseball and most local players were part-time professionals. Not all the games were on grass, either. The two games against an All-Star British Columbia side were played at Vancouver on Callister Park's notorious dirt pitch. The first match ended in a 4-4 draw, but in the second the England FA won 7-1, running away with six goals in the second half – three each from Jimmy Hagan and Stoke City's Frank Bowyer.

The programme also included a Test match in New York versus an American Soccer League XI (essentially the USA World Cup team which two weeks later beat England in the World Cup). The England FA won their match 1-0.

The trip was a welcome escape from the hardships of post-war Britain. It offered no great financial rewards but players did receive a cap at the end of the tour. Among the guidance notes for players was the following:

> Under present currency regulations, no individual may take out of the country more than £5 sterling. It is not permissible to spend any of this amount whilst abroad. Arrangements have been made to provide members of the party with an allowance of $6 per day from the date of embarkation until the date of disembarkation.
>
> Each player is expected to pay the following personal expenses from the allowance given to him: personal laundry; telegrams; cleaning and pressing of suits; long distance calls; room radio service at hotel.
>
> No bonuses will be paid in respect of matches played.
>
> Shorts, stockings and numbered shirts will be provided by The Football Association. Players should take with them athletic slips, gym shoes, shin guards, spikes and football boots.

Around this time Hagan gave up any thoughts of obtaining a professional qualification outside football and started a business venture with his fellow inside forward, Harold Brook. The pair opened a sports outfitters' shop at 108 London Road, appropriately called Hagan and Brook. These were the days before club shops – and indeed replica kits – but many a schoolboy went along to the shop to buy a red and white shirt, black shorts and a pair of football boots. The shop was very much a hands-on venture for the two owners, and Hagan took pains to ensure that customers were satisfied. Years later a message from a fan on a greetings card for Hagan's eightieth birthday said it all:

> I came in to buy a new pair of football boots and you insisted on personally fitting me out. Eventually you finished up selling me a size 9 for the left foot and a size 8 for the right foot. I recall Harold being less than pleased and his final observation: 'I don't know who the bloody hell we're going to sell the other two odd ones to.'

CHAPTER NINE

Into the Fifties

By the early 1950s Jimmy, Iris and their son, David, were happily installed in a house which belonged to the club, at 71 Hollythorpe Road, Sheffield 8. By the standards of the time he was reasonably well off and was one of the few people in the area to own a car. Footballers were still restricted to the maximum wage rules, but Jimmy was careful with his money, and his other business interests provided welcome additional income.

The Sheffield United board minutes dated 27 July 1950 contain a significant entry, noting that Hagan had signed full-time terms at a weekly wage of £12 (£10 in the summer). This was the Football League maximum at the time, and a handful of Jimmy's senior colleagues received the same amount.

He supplemented his income with articles for the local and national media, always writing them himself, and never using a ghost writer. He would draft the articles out in his neat handwriting and Iris would type them up for him. He wrote well, and was not afraid to tackle controversial issues. One such article appeared in the weekly magazine *Tit Bits* on 11 April 1950:

Abolish the Off-Side Rule by Jimmy Hagan
Without doubt the biggest bug-bear in the game is off-side. Generations of players have complained about it. The rule itself is complicated and

unwieldy. We have all seen apparently good goals disallowed because the referee or linesmen think the off side rule has been broken. On the other hand we have all seen cases where defenders stop playing and appeal for off-side while an opponent goes on to score a goal which is allowed.

It is unfair to both players and officials. The teams never know for certain whether the referee is going to whistle or not when there is a hairline case. And the official who is doing his duty by keeping up with play is often not at the proper angle to decide accurately.

A player can be on-side when the ball is sent to him. But while it is in motion the defenders move upfield so that when the pass reaches him he is yards off-side. Nine times out of ten the whistle blows. It is no consolation to the attacking side, or their supporters, to know that the referee had made a mistake. That's when the arguments start!

How can incidents like this be avoided? There is one very simple way. Don't just tamper with the off-side rule. Abolish it altogether.

What would happen if there were no off-side in football? More goals, of course, since none would be disallowed for this 'crime'. The game would also improve as a spectacle.

The spectators pay to see good football plus excitement in the goalmouth. The off-side rule puts a brake on both. There can be few thrills in front of goal if the attack peters out near the penalty area. I maintain that too much mid-field play makes a game uninteresting and leads to too many goalless draws.

Readers may argue that abolition of off-side would mean that forwards would lie well upfield. Well, what's wrong with that? There might be more of those long passes from the backs to the forwards that we all like to see and which turn defence into attack and so open up the game.

The changes would put defenders on their mettle. They would have to mark forwards closely and work out clever defensive schemes. There's nothing clever in stepping a yard or two up and yelling 'Off-side!' hoping the referee agrees.

…I feel very strongly that if forwards manage to out-manoeuvre defenders by good football movements they should not be held up by the off-side law. Defenders should counter good passing and good positional play by close marking, clever interception and anticipation.

What does it matter if there are more goals? The high number of goals scored in ice-hockey certainly do not detract from the merits of the game – either as a sport or a spectacle. Goals are what the crowd go to cheer, and I don't know a defender worth his salt who would not prefer to stop an opposing forward by his own skill than by appealing to the whistle.

…Another change I should like to see to give spectators their money's worth would be a revision of the law which deals with the duration of the game. The actual playing period should be ninety minutes. And time taken up by all stoppages, whether for injuries or the ball being out of play, should not be counted as part of the match.

I have often thought what a pity it is that a team that keeps kicking the ball out of play cannot be penalized. If a throw-in counted against a team in the final result, players would think twice before belting the ball out of the ground.

…I think many officials pay too much attention to trivialities and not enough to important issues… I have an unhappy memory of one referee's failure to notice a glaring case. Our rivals were pressing and I was in the penalty area. As the ball came across an opponent handled it, so blatantly that I was sure the whistle had gone.

I picked the ball up to place it for the free-kick to us. Then the referee whistled and pointed to the penalty spot. He hadn't seen the first handling but he had noticed me doing it! The penalty kick was converted into a goal and we lost 2-3. Now I have my own rule. I keep playing till the whistle goes!

Iris and David attended all the home matches. Iris was a nervous spectator, forever worried that Jimmy would get injured, and her voice could be heard, shouting instructions to her husband. If he could have heard her above the noise of the crowd (which is most unlikely) he would have ignored her, just as he ignored all other advice. Iris' favourite refrain was 'Get rid of it Jimmy!' She wasn't interested in Jimmy's skill and trickery on the ball – just worried that someone would get him with a scything tackle. In fact, she need not have worried unduly, for Jimmy was well able to skip over most tackles.

His normal routine, following a home game, was to sign autographs for all the youngsters who waited outside the players' entrance. At such times the sergeant major in him would manifest itself. He would not tolerate any jostling by the autograph hunters, but would insist that they line up and wait their turn. He would then patiently sign every autograph that was requested of him, however long it took. His view was 'if they have taken the trouble to wait for me, it is only right that I give them a little of my time'. Meanwhile Iris and David had to wait patiently for this ritual to end. Then he would drive his family straight home for tea.

Although he did not smoke or drink, he still had time for his teammates, many of whom would gather in the Nelson pub after the game for a few drinks. Hagan would sometimes drive back into town to join them in the pub, and there he would enjoy the banter and crack a few jokes over his soft drink.

Fans who only knew Jimmy as the poker-faced player on the pitch could have been forgiven for thinking that he didn't care about the result of matches, but, in fact, he enjoyed the successes and was bitterly disappointed by the failures. His young son, David, learned to keep out of his father's way after a match if the team had lost badly.

Jimmy's persona to the public was never less than professional. He was a popular figure on the 'Soccer Viewpoints' football panels, presented by the Sheffield newspapers, when he was, as one journalist remembered, 'an outstanding personality, thoughtful in his treatment of football problems, but oft-times with an irrepressible humour bubbling from within.'

Jimmy was immaculately dressed on such occasions, always wearing a tie and usually a blazer with his England badge on it.

Derek Dooley remembers appearing on panels and at social events with Hagan in the early 1950s. Dooley was then a goal machine for Sheffield Wednesday (he once scored five in a single match) but off the field he was a shy youth, unused to speaking in public. By contrast, the experienced Hagan seemed confident and at ease in such situations and could always find the right words, and a joke or two. Jimmy was invariably kind to the youngster and helped guide him through the ordeals. Today, Derek says he has many happy memories of Jimmy socially and adds, 'I am proud to think that I was one of his friends.'

Despite the legendary rivalry between Blades and Owls fans, the players of the two Sheffield clubs often met socially and got on well together. Cricket matches between Sheffield United and Sheffield Wednesday were organised in the summer where the Blades' partnership of Hagan and Brook often excelled.

Hagan readily agreed to play in Dooley's testimonial match after Derek's career was tragically cut short in 1953.

There was another side to Hagan, though. He could be a stickler for respect and discipline, even from his adoring fans. One bonfire night some children from his neighbourhood were passing the Hagan house on Hollythorpe Road when he was having a bonfire and fireworks party. Hagan generously invited the children in to enjoy the occasion, but when one of the boys called him Jimmy it brought a frosty response: 'Mr Hagan to you'.

If 1949/50 had been a little unproductive, Jimmy got his appetite back for goals in the 1950/51 season, scoring 17 from 40 appearances, but the team got off to a bad start and never recovered. Centre forward was a problem position all season and injuries made it difficult to maintain a settled team. The arrival of two wingers – Derek Hawksworth and Alf Ringstead – during the season promised much for the future, however. United finished the season in eighth place in the Second Division.

Meanwhile Sheffield Wednesday were having their own problems in the First Division and at the beginning of February 1951 made an audacious transfer bid of £32,500 for Hagan, who was by now thirty-three years old. Hagan told the Owls' secretary-manager Eric Taylor, 'You surely wouldn't think of paying all that money for a player of my age, would you?' Taylor replied, 'I think you are just the man to pull us together for a few years if you come to Hillsborough.'

The Owls wanted Hagan to play alongside Derek Dooley and the United board jumped at the offer, deciding in a vote of 9-2 that such a huge fee would be a fair return for the loss of their top player and talisman. The two clubs agreed the deal, subject to Hagan's acceptance, but Wednesday insisted on an immediate decision so that Jimmy could play in the following Saturday's game. The news hit the Sheffield public like a bombshell and there was talk of little else. Had it gone through, the transfer would have been a new British record. It would also have split the city down the middle for Hagan was regarded as irreplaceable at Bramall Lane. Hagan told the Wednesday management that he would think about it, whilst tens of thousands of Blades fans held their breath.

Finally, after giving it a great deal of thought he politely declined the offer. Whatever reasons he gave, we don't know, but he told his family that he would not have been able to hold his head up in the city had he moved to Hillsborough. Financially, of course, it would have had little benefit for Hagan. Wages were still limited to a fixed maximum and players did not receive big signing-on fees. However, being in the First Division shop window could have helped his chances of getting an England recall.

Another factor might have been that Hagan needed to have an operation on his left thumb. United had agreed for him to have time off in late season for this to be done so that he could take up an invitation by the FA to go on a tour of Australia during the summer. Had he moved to Hillsborough he would have been required to complete the season and would have had to pull out of the Australian tour.

Some years later he said: 'One of the reasons I declined to move across the city is that I have never thought any footballer was worth £32,500, and definitely not at thirty-three.'

Hagan did not endear himself to some members of the Sheffield United board by turning down the transfer, and the two clubs tried to keep the deal alive. The chairmen had another discussion towards the end of February when Wednesday now said that the offer of £32,500 'no longer held good' although they would still like to talk to Hagan again. The United board did not agree and the matter appears to have ended there.

The furore did provoke interest from other clubs, however, and Wolves offered the raven-haired centre forward Jesse Pye in part-exchange for Hagan, but the board said no.

Sheffield Wednesday did break the transfer record shortly after Hagan turned them down. In March 1951 they signed Jackie Sewell from Notts County for £34,000.

Jimmy had the operation on his thumb at the beginning of April, which involved a short stay in Sheffield's Royal Hospital, and he missed the final six League games for Sheffield United. Hagan's absence probably had little bearing on United's promotion chances since the team finished well adrift of the top places.

Then came the FA tour of Australia, an ambitious programme involving players being away from their families for nearly three months. The eighteen-strong party contained no current internationals, perhaps in recognition of the lower standard of competition down under, for association football was not as well developed in Australia in 1951 as it is now. Nevertheless, the squad contained many players who could be regarded as on the fringe of the England team. Along with Jimmy were two of his Sheffield United teammates, Ted Burgin (goalkeeper) and Joe Shaw, who at that time was a wing half. Also in the squad was Jackie Sewell of Sheffield Wednesday.

Meeting up with the squad for the first time at the Great Western Hotel, Paddington, Jimmy was pleased to note that one of the two co-managers of the tour was an old colleague from his wartime football: Wing Commander Adams who had looked after the services team on the Continent during the war. He noted that everyone seemed to get on well during that first evening and looked forward to an enjoyable tour.

It was a gruelling trip by modern standards, flying first by Stratocruiser to New York (where they played a match against a local side), and then via San Francisco, Honolulu, Fiji and Canton Island to Sydney.

The team was in Australia for all of ten weeks and played 21 games, including five Test matches against Australia. They won them all easily, the scoreline in two of the non-Test matches being 17-0! It must have been a pleasant break from post-war Britain, where rationing was still in force – five years after the war had been won – and Jimmy received another cap to add to his collection.

He wrote a detailed account of the tour – perhaps with a view to publication on his return – but modestly refrained from giving any details of his goals. Nor did he dwell on the fact that he was one of the major stars of the tour, his ball control and distribution on the often bone-hard grounds amazing the local crowds. Raymond Glendenning subsequently wrote that Hagan 'proved the big success of the FA team's 21-match tour of Australia'.

Joe Shaw later recalled that Hagan acted like a father to his Sheffield United teammates on the tour. Unlike Hagan, most of the players enjoyed a drink and made full use of the bars on their travels. Hagan would keep an eye on Shaw and Burgin to see that they came to no harm and ensured that the players were back in their hotel rooms at a reasonable hour. One might assume that Hagan – a lifelong teetotaller – would disapprove of his fellow professionals having a few (or, in some cases, rather too many) drinks, but Jimmy never told tales.

There were moments of controversy, however. With frequent stops in a variety of hotels around Australia, the party needed places that provided suitable rest and relaxation for them to recover from their rigorous schedule. In Melbourne they moved hotels when they found themselves booked into a very busy, popular hotel, with cramped rooms. They found a smaller hotel nearby more to their liking.

When they reached Hobart, Tasmania, the visitors found that the accommodation wasn't at all suitable, so they immediately moved to a luxurious hotel right on the waterfront, with a swimming pool – the nicest hotel of their whole trip, according to Hagan. Someone told the local press and soon the story was going around that the Poms were not satisfied with one of Hobart's best hotels. Indignant letters appeared in the papers (including one from the mayor) inferring that the footballers were snobs. The players were gagged by the team management and not allowed to explain what was wrong with the first hotel so they had to grin and bear it. Feelings ran so high that some Hobart inhabitants sprinkled broken glass on the playing pitch before the planned football game against the city side. The game could have been called off, but to avoid a diplomatic incident the glass was cleared up and the game was eventually played. In wet conditions the England side got on with the job and they won the match comprehensively, 11-0.

A couple of days later, in a match against a Tasmania State side, in front of a crowd of 2,500, Hagan inspired the English FA side to a 17-0 win. Hagan scored eight goals in this match, setting an individual Australian record. After all the bad publicity it seems the team decided to put the Tasmanians firmly in their place and gave a dazzling display of attacking football which saw the visitors six goals up in the first fifteen minutes. Perhaps the fact that Jackie Sewell, Hagan's Sheffield rival, had scored seven goals in a match just eleven days earlier provided an additional spur for Jimmy to go one better. Sam Bartram, who was in goal for this match, must have had one of the easiest games of his illustrious career!

During the tour the team had time to relax on the beaches and do some sightseeing, of course, and were invited to numerous civic receptions, and even an informal rabbit shoot at one point. Travel was by plane, train and bus. A visit to the industrial town of Wollangong, New South Wales, interested Hagan particularly, for most of the inhabitants were former miners from Northumberland and Durham who had emigrated to Australia after the war. They had been looking forward to this match for months. Hagan wrote that his side ran out winners 7-0 and pleased the crowd with some well-worked goals.

On their return to Sydney, however, their bus broke down and they eventually arrived back at their hotel, tired and hungry, at 2a.m.

The long Australian tour must have left its participants in good physical shape for the new season and 1951/52 started brilliantly for Sheffield United for whom Hagan had been restored to the captaincy, and was now the beneficiary of £14 per week – the new Football League maximum wage. By the end of October the results were: played 14, won 10, drawn 2, lost 2. This period included a record 7-3 victory over Sheffield Wednesday (who had returned to the Second Division after just one season in the top flight) at Bramall Lane. The purple patch also saw the team score six against West Ham and five against both Blackburn Rovers and Swansea Town.

On 22 September Fred Walters wrote in the *Green 'Un*:

Jimmy Hagan – one of the few football artists of the game, is now proving an out and out captain – a player to remind one of the great inside forwards like Clem Stephenson, Billy Gillespie, Jimmy Seed, Billy Walker, Joe Smith and the others of bygone days. As a captain he is there to lead and dictate the type of game best suited to the occasion… United have it within them to win promotion this season.

However, it was not to be. The turning point came in a remarkable 5-5 draw away at Leicester City on 3 November in which Hagan starred. A report of the match said:

Jimmy Baldwin, Leicester's wiry little right half tried hard to obey his manager's instructions to pin down Hagan, yet must have spent the weekend contemplating the two goals scored by the irrepressible United forward, and the tenth goal which Hagan inspired and Smith scored six minutes from the end.

Of all the wonderful goals on an afternoon of sharp shooting, none was more superb than Hagan's first. He gained possession about 20 yards out, halted and invited Leicester to take it off him. Leicester

declined. Hagan feinted, made a left side-step with the ball, and drove
it hard into the roof of the net with his left foot.

In later years Hagan said that this was his favourite match as a player.
He always believed that football should be entertaining and would
much rather see a game end 5-5 than 0-0. Blades who eagerly bought
the *Green 'Un* following the Leicester City game, expecting banner
headlines for their team on the front page, were disappointed. Across
the city the remarkable scoring machine that was Derek Dooley had
scored five!

After this, the team rather lost its way and gradually slipped down the
table. The defence, in particular, was chopped and changed too much.
Hagan was out injured with a severe knee injury for a couple of months
in the middle of the season, during which the team won only four out
of 13 matches, but in truth they did not fare much better after Hagan's
return. Harold Brook, too, was injured from the beginning of February
until the end of the season. He had scored 17 goals in 27 games up to
his injury, which shows what might have been. Alf Ringstead, however,
was banging the goals in all season, and managed 27 – a remarkable total
for a winger. Hagan played 32 games in all competitions and scored 12
goals. Harry Hitchen took over the captaincy when Hagan was injured
in November, and retained it until the end of the season, but whenever
Hagan was playing, he was the inspiration for the whole team.

Sheffield Wednesday were promoted again (leading to comments in the press about the 'Sheffield yo-yo') and United finished
mid-table in a disappointing eleventh place.

The FA Cup that season provided one of those special 'Hagan
moments' when he rose above even his own impeccable standards.
The occasion was the fourth round, with United playing away at
West Ham on 2 February 1952. It was Hagan's first match back after
a two-month lay off with his knee injury.

The pitch was a mudbath and it was not a great game of football,
but after centre half Harry Latham pulled a muscle after thirty minutes
and was a virtual passenger for the rest of the match, Hagan reshuffled

the team. The limping Latham went to centre forward, Joe Shaw to centre half and Hagan dropped back, nominally to left half, but he was here, there and everywhere, always on the move, plugging gaps and inspiring his colleagues. Everyone agreed that he kept United in the cup. With fifteen minutes to go Hagan turned up on the right wing and very nearly won the match with a characteristic Hagan run.

All the newspapers were full of praise for Hagan's leadership. 'What a difference a Hagan makes', 'Hagan shows his genius as wing half', 'Hagan was hero in mudbath', 'Hagan was star of injury-hit side', and 'It was Hagan-inspired' were some of the headlines.

Joe Shaw, too, had a great match at centre half – a position that he was to make his own some years later.

United gained a well-earned 0-0 draw, and a replay, which saw them defeat West Ham at home 4-2 four days later with another Hagan virtuoso performance.

A month before he sustained his serious knee injury it seems Hagan was on the verge of an England recall if one is to believe an article in the *Evening Chronicle* of 13 October 1951 by John Graydon. He wrote:

> Do not be shocked if Jimmy Hagan, after so long out of the international spotlight, is recalled. In my view the selection of Hagan would be an excellent one. He can 'general' an attack, has the ability to bring the best out of the players with whom he is working, and as one of Soccer's 'big names' would undoubtedly have a great influence upon his colleagues.
>
> This season Hagan is playing well. On form he is undoubtedly the best inside-forward in the country. I hope the selectors share my view – I have reason to believe some of them do – and Hagan, a truly great footballer, is recalled.

It was an eloquent plea by Graydon (and he was by no means alone in his views), but the selectors did not recall Hagan to the England side. Just how close he came to another England cap at that point one can only guess.

CHAPTER TEN

Promotion

For the 1952/53 campaign, despite the disappointments of the previous season, the nucleus of a good side was there and this was sensibly built on by a new manager, Reg Freeman (formerly with Rotherham United), who took over from Teddy Davison during the close season. The teenage Graham Shaw became a regular fixture in the side at left-back. Harold Brook played a virtually complete injury-free season. Hawksworth and Ringstead were on top form on the wings, and Hagan had one of his best seasons ever for the Blades. Len Browning, at centre forward, came into his own and had a great season, too. United managed to keep a relatively settled side throughout, and when changes had to be made, the replacements did their job well. The captaincy was shared between Harry Hitchen and Harold Brook, but Hagan remained the focal point of the team.

In June 1952 the club had received a request from Rochdale to talk to Hagan with a view to his becoming the club's player-manager, but the board – sensibly for once – refused.

Hagan did put in a request to the board at the beginning of August for a benefit clause to be inserted into his contract. Benefit payments were common for long-serving players and presumably Hagan had missed out on this clause when he had a part-time contract. Approval should have been a formality for their star player but – bizarrely – the board rejected his request at their meeting of 8 August 1952. One can only wonder what they were thinking of, but it was presumably the money that they could save.

The matter was raised again at a board meeting two months later, this time by the manager, Reg Freeman, who presumably spoke up forcefully for Hagan since it was agreed and Jimmy was assured of his benefit.

Privately, Hagan was often scathing in his views of the Sheffield United board, whose members he regarded as knowing little about football (a view that he held of football clubs' chairmen and board members in general). Football was still ruled by a feudal system where players were kept in their place by the management, and the Football League with its strict maximum wage rules, so Hagan was not alone.

From the start in August 1952 the team hit form and they maintained it consistently through the season, moving to the top of the League in November and staying there to win the league with 60 points (equivalent to 86 in today's terms). The 42 League games produced no fewer than 97 goals, so the fans had plenty to celebrate. Including cup games, Hagan scored 20, Alf Ringstead and Len Browning each scored 23, Harold Brook 17 and Derek Hawksworth 13. The whole forward line thus reached double figures. For all the team it meant a Second Division Championship medal, and Hagan proudly added this to his collection of international and representative medals.

Hagan, traditionally an inside left, was switched by Reg Freeman to inside right from the beginning of October, with the inside left spot being taken mostly by Harold Brook – who, of course, had traditionally been an inside right. Whatever the thinking was behind this move, it worked, and this line-up remained throughout most of the season. As far as Hagan was concerned the line-up was academic, for he would never be tied down in one position, and could turn up almost anywhere to make a telling contribution or embarrass the opposition.

Hagan had so many great games that it would be tedious to record them all, but all the press were full of praise for the 2–2 home draw against Birmingham City on 25 October. One journalist asked:

How does he do it? How, at 33 this talented footballer can at one moment make goal chances at one end of the field, and seemingly in the next moment pull his side from a tough spot at the other end; then take a throw-in on one side of the field, and almost immediately one across at the other.

The Bramall Lane crowd seem to take Hagan for granted; to me he is a delight to watch – a player with the equipment of the complete footballer and the surprise element thrown in.

On 8 November 1952, United played Southampton at Bramall Lane and Hagan produced yet another of his virtuoso performances. United won 5-3 and Hagan scored a hat-trick with three cracking goals, proving – as one newspaper said – that he was not 'too old for England'. It was more than thirteen years since Hagan's previous League hat-trick, achieved in that memorable 6-1 defeat of Spurs in May 1939.

Two weeks later Leicester City came to Bramall Lane with a strong attack, led by Arthur Rowley, and a reputation as a goal-minded side. They went away thoroughly crushed by a 7-2 defeat. Jimmy Hagan was the architect of the demolition job and helped himself to two of the goals.

A little later came an incident which has never been forgotten by Blades fans who were present on that day. Sheffield United played Swansea Town at home on 20 December 1952 and by half-time were 3-0 up and well in command. Referees were more tolerant of physical play in those days and many teams of that era had a 'clogger' – a player who relished a strong tackle and who would try to kick the opposition's key players into submission. Swansea had a wing half called Lucas, a dark-haired stocky character who, in football parlance, 'put himself about a bit'. It is said that there was some history between him and Hagan.

From the start Lucas set out to reduce Hagan's influence by a succession of niggling fouls. Hagan was used to this, and he knew how to skip out of the way of flying tackles. However, as the game went on, and the goals kept going into the Swansea net, Lucas' tackles became ever more crude and the referee did very little to stop the onslaught.

Towards the end of the game, after Hagan had scored United's seventh goal, Lucas made one more scything tackle on Hagan, who picked himself up off the floor and appeared to aim a short, sharp kick at Lucas' leg. This was so uncharacteristic of Hagan that the spectators could hardly believe their eyes. His foot travelled only a short distance and seemed more of a gesture of annoyance than a full-blooded kick. It is questionable, in fact, whether the kick even landed on its target, but Lucas went down as though hit by a sniper's bullet and rolled around in apparent agony.

Red and yellow cards had not been introduced to the game in 1952, and misdemeanours were dealt with by the referee taking a player's name. Sending-offs were rare.

Many onlookers – including those in the press box – expected the referee to take action against Lucas for the initial tackle and were surprised when he called Hagan over to him. A discussion took place and after a few moments the fans watched in disbelief as Hagan trudged, head bowed, towards the touchline. He had been sent off! The remaining minutes of the game took place in a chorus of boos as the fans vented their anger on the referee. The media thought that Hagan must have said something to the referee, for they felt the incident did not warrant a sending off, but apparently the referee later confirmed that he had sent Jimmy off for retaliation.

By the time the rest of the team trooped into the dressing room at the end of the game Hagan had recovered his dry sense of humour. He was already in the bath and quipped 'Did you manage to hang on then?' United had won 7-1.

The club backed Hagan and asked the FA for Jimmy to have a personal hearing, sending board member Mr L. Lewis to accompany him at the meeting at the Grand Hotel, Birmingham on 8 January 1953. The result was that Jimmy was cautioned by the FA but not suspended, so it seems that common sense prevailed.

In later years Hagan was always reluctant to talk about the incident, even to his own family, but here's how one local journalist recorded it a few days after the match:

There was pandemonium when Hagan was sent off the field. That was to be expected – for extreme partisanship is inseparable from League football – especially when the victim of the penalty commands the admiration of the multitude to the extent that Hagan does.

I was in what may be described as a more impartial atmosphere – in the seats for visitors. None of the visitors, like myself, saw any action in the play to justify the drastic decision. We all assumed that Hagan had been (shall I say?), indiscreet in his comments to the referee when the official asked his name.

But I have since heard that the player, apart from giving his name to the official, said nothing.

I am mystified. Thousands just as near the scene are no doubt equally puzzled… a referee must act according to what he sees or thinks he sees.

Whether, in fact, this official might have been influenced subconsciously by the histrionic antics of one of the Swansea players I cannot say. Certainly that man was restored to complete health and mobility within a remarkably short period.

This was the only blemish of the season for Hagan who scored his 100th League goal against Blackburn on 21 February 1953. In fact, it was the only black mark in his career, which probably explains why he was reluctant to discuss it.

Virtually every week the match reports in newspapers singled out Hagan for special praise. 'General Hagan will lead to Div.1 – His Finest Season', 'Hagan Gives A Masterly Exhibition', 'Genius Jimmy shows United the way back to Div. 1 football', and 'Hagan Still A Genius' were typical of the headlines, week in and week out. The fans who witnessed this remarkable season were indeed fortunate, for such treats do not come along very often – for Sheffield United followers, at least.

The 1952/53 season had been a triumph for all the Sheffield United players, but none more so than Jimmy Hagan who was thirty-five by the time the season ended but still playing as well as ever. Now he could look forward to parading his skills on the First Division stage for the first time since 1949.

He may have been out of favour with the England selectors but he had his supporters amongst the media. Raymond Glendenning's *Book of Sport for Boys*, published at the start of 1953, selected the following 'Eleven Outstanding Footballers of 1952–53' for his 'Winning Team': Sam Bartram, Harry Johnston, Ron Burgess, George Young, Tommy Docherty, Lionel Smith, Stanley Matthews, Nat Lofthouse, Don Roper, Frank Blunstone and Jimmy Hagan. Jimmy and Raymond Glendenning had known each other since the war years, of course.

There was still a feeling amongst fans and some of the local media that Hagan *was* Sheffield United, to the extent that the local sports paper, the *Green 'Un*, once doctored a team photograph of Sheffield United to show eleven Jimmy Hagans. The joke went down well amongst Hagan's legions of fans, although understandably some of the players were not so amused. If Hagan himself privately enjoyed the accolade he would have made light of it in front of his teammates, for it was not in his nature to gloat.

By modern standards, Jimmy Hagan was nothing less than a superstar, although in the days before the widespread use of television, celebrity status was harder to achieve. He was regularly called a 'football genius' by the media and the Blades fans adored him, but still he remained a quiet, modest and private man. An article written in the magazine *Raich Carter's Soccer Star* in February 1953 by Lee Norris opened with the words:

> You talk to him and find he's quieter than most footballers. When the Sheffield United team are in a hotel he sits on his own at times, a serious, dark, handsome young man. In a bus he is the boy who likes to sit back and read a newspaper. He is Jimmy Hagan, the idol of those Sheffield folks who prefer Bramall Lane to Hillsborough. He is the quietest, shrewdest man kicking a ball about.

The article also contained an excellent appraisal of Hagan's unique skills, which will evoke fond memories in all those who were fortunate enough to see him play:

He is one of the game's greats. No one has ever been able to trap a ball like Hagan. Many have done it as well but it doesn't LOOK the same. Hagan doesn't have to look when he traps a ball. He spots the way he's going to do it, then as the ball drops towards his foot, the dark eyes are flashing about the field and in one movement the ball is controlled and dispatched. Just like that.

…Jimmy has that touch of uniqueness that makes him a star. Alex James had it in that devastating swerve; Tommy Lawton in the graceful arched way he got up to head a ball; Wilf Mannion in the pretty way he held his hands out at the sides and ran his foot over the ball; Stan Matthews with the magic that you can't pin down to any one thing.

With Hagan it is the trap. When other things are forgotten about Hagan, and when we are grandfathers proclaiming hotly that football ain't what it used to be, we will tell our squalling grandchildren that if you're talking about Billy Bloggs being a great trapper, you should have seen Hagan.

…He is pretty to watch. He can do the impossible. A high ball swings in from the right wing. Mr Hagan is placed as awkwardly as he can be (thanks to the opposing defence) with his back to goal. The ball comes in waist high. The defence dithers and wonders. Mr Hagan doesn't. He swings round and wham, somehow that ball is in the back of the net.

Or he can dribble. A loose wild clearance to the centre spot. Mr Hagan fastens on to the ball. The United line moves up, watching the fluttering feet, the casual body swerve. The defence moves backwards, looking at Hagan and the rest of the United line cautiously out of the corners of their eyes.

Mr Hagan is making ground all the time. Then, too late, the defence realises that Mr Hagan is not going to flick the ball out to a forward colleague. He's going through himself.

Too late. Mr Hagan is there. So is the ball. In the net.

Heartbreak Hagan they call him… when you're on the other side. And perhaps when you are on the same side. For Jimmy makes a good player look ordinary; the team-mates suffer from comparison.

…It is not only the footballing prowess of Hagan that has inspired United. It is the example and the inspiration his presence gives.

He is the rock of Sheffield United, the foundation of a footballing team.

…There are those amongst us who say a lot of rude things about Jimmy.

Too casual. Boloney

Too pretty-pretty. Poppycock

Too good. Dead right.

CHAPTER ELEVEN

Top Flight Again

As the 1953/54 season approached Hagan relished the challenge of playing again in the First Division and was reported to be 'training as he has never trained before'. The board even agreed, in September 1953, to play 'Wonderful, Wonderful Copenhagen' at matches on the club's newly installed loudspeaker system (the tune had been adapted by the fans, who sang 'Wonderful, Wonderful Jimmy Hagan'). Sadly the new system also marked the end of the live brass band at matches, although the club kept up tradition by playing brass band music via the loudspeakers.

Meanwhile the manager, Reg Freeman, boosted the playing staff with several signings, among them a nineteen-year-old winger, Colin Grainger, from Wrexham. He and the slightly-built inside forward Peter Wragg (who joined midway through the promotion season) both made their mark in the First Division. Jim's pal and business partner, Harold Brook, remained as captain.

Sheffield United spent the next three seasons in the First Division, maintaining, with their rivals across the city, the yo-yo effect. The 1953/54 season was a struggle, although the team started quite well, picking up four wins and a draw in the first seven games.

The opening match augured well for the future, with United beating Portsmouth away from home in a 4-3 thriller. Again it was that man Hagan who dominated the sports pages. Clifford Webb wrote:

You couldn't help liking the look of Sheffield United and you could hardly refrain from being amazed at the energy and industry of Jimmy Hagan, who must now be quite tired of trying to convince the selectors that he is far from the bathchair stage.

For me Jimmy was the man of the match. In possession, he was virtually unstoppable.

A 1-0 win over the reigning League Champions, Arsenal, followed and in the return match at Highbury just one week later, United held the Gunners to a 1-1 draw, the home team equalising with a lucky deflection off the young Graham Shaw.

A few days later United had to play another high-flying team, Chelsea, at Stamford Bridge. Chelsea dominated the first hour and Ted Burgin was brilliant in goal. Then Hagan turned on his magic, scoring both United's goals in a 2-1 victory. 'Chelsea surprised by Hagan', 'Chelsea Beaten by Hagan', and 'Brilliant Hagan and Burgin Foil Chelsea' said the headlines. One of the Sunday papers described Hagan's second goal: 'Juggler Jimmy tricked centre-half Jack Saunders, drew 'keeper Robertson out, showed him the ball and then cheekily whipped it away to shoot past full-back Willemse into the spot that counts.' The England manager, Walter Winterbottom, was present, and even slipped into the United dressing room to commend Hagan for his performance, but it seems nothing Hagan could do would earn him an England recall.

Hughie Gallagher described Jimmy Hagan in his weekly column as:

...one of the old school, when footwork had to be allied to brainwork and spirit. Today, things are different. There's far too much slackness in the inside berths, and too half-hearted an approach to tackling. Now forwards seem content to stand back to camera-posing distance when an opposing defender is in possession. Alas, the race of players with sound positional sense has almost disappeared... Nowadays craftsmen are few; the labourers many. That's why Jimmy Hagan, a diamond among pebbles, continues to shine and continues to be talked of as an England 'possible' this season.

On 12 September 1953 United met the old enemy, Sheffield Wednesday, at Bramall Lane, the first time the two clubs had met in the First Division for nineteen years. The Blades demolished the Owls 2-0 with Hagan and Hawksworth scoring the goals in front of a crowd of 45,463. The match, like so many local derbies, did not serve up great football, but Hagan was one of the few bright spots, despite the fact that he had been nursing an injury and only made a last-minute decision to play. Wednesday had a young keeper in goal for the first time and Hagan tested him severely, shooting every time he was in range.

Kenneth Wolstenholme wrote in one of the Sunday papers:

> Hagan can justly claim he has been robbed if the England selectors refuse to reward his brilliance with a cap. He simply strolled through the game, which he commanded as firmly as any battleship captain. Whenever he had the ball, something happened; no one could match his control, no one could dispute his mastery.

There's no doubt that there was widespread support for Hagan to be recalled to the England side, despite the fact that he was thirty-six in February 1954. That same month his picture was on the cover of the popular journal *Charles Buchan's Football Monthly*, with the caption: 'Jimmy Hagan, Sheffield United and England'. If this was a hint in the direction of the England selectors, it fell on deaf ears.

Sadly, Len Browning, the centre forward who had been so influential in the promotion year, played only six matches before he fell ill with tuberculosis and eventually had to give up the game. Browning's shoes were difficult to fill and after the good start United lost six and drew one out of their next seven games, and the rest of the season was dire, apart from a little flurry of wins in late November and early December (when Hagan was actually out injured). The team just avoided relegation, finishing twentieth out of the twenty-two teams. Sheffield Wednesday were not much better, finishing one place above United. Hagan, who missed more than a third of the season through injury, was forced to play a deeper, midfield role and scored just eight goals from 30 games, and two of these were in a County Cup match against Rotherham.

By now Jimmy must have been thinking of staying in the game after his playing days were over for, in April 1954, he attended an FA coaching course along with Albert Cox, the United full-back. Not all would-be coaches were top professional footballers, of course, and during sessions that involved knocking a ball back and forth to a partner, some of the others would lose control of their ball. If a stray ball came his way Jimmy amazed the other participants by his uncanny knack of catching the ball on his foot and returning it unerringly whence it came, all in one movement. Out of thirty-seven participants in the Sheffield region, only eleven passed the course and Hagan was one of them. Among the failures were a couple of well-known professional footballers!

The Sheffield United board discussed the possibility of offering Hagan a coaching role in October 1954, but there was no clear agreement and the matter was deferred for the time being. The board did agree, in November, to approach the Football League for permission to pay Hagan a full benefit of £750.

On the field, the 1954/55 season was much better for United. The supposedly injury-prone Harold Brook had been sold to Leeds United (where he proceeded to show that he was far from finished), but the pacey Colin Grainger stepped up from being a bit-part player to justify a regular place on the right wing, and eventually played for England. Grainger's pace and good control combined well with Hagan's sublime skills to open up defences. Jack Cross did a decent job in the centre forward role and Joe Shaw was made captain and moved to centre half from his former wing half position, where he proved to be outstanding, despite his lack of inches. Ringstead and Hawksworth were their usual effective selves, although the latter became something of a utility player, appearing in all forward positions except inside left during the course of the season. In Jim Iley and Tommy Hoyland, the team had two excellent wing halves to provide some authority in midfield.

Hagan was still capable of turning in match-winning performances, even against the best opposition. Sheffield United played

Manchester United on 14 November 1954 at Bramall Lane, and for a time most of the traffic was one way, with Ted Burgin making some valiant saves to keep the Blades in the match. In the second half, however, the tide swung the other way and for the last twenty-five minutes Hagan inspired a match-winning rally, the Blades scoring three goals in thirteen minutes. First, Colin Grainger netted from a difficult angle after seventy minutes; then a long kick from Burgin caught out the Manchester defence and Jack Cross nipped in to score from long range.

Seven minutes from time, Joe Shaw sent a long ball out of defence. The *Sunday Pictorial* described what happened next: 'Hagan, that astute master, seeing the Manchester defence so well up, ran from his own half and, from twenty yards lobbed the ball over the head of the advancing goalkeeper. The way in which he did the whole thing was the coolest thing imaginable.' The story speaks volumes for Hagan's fitness, at the age of nearly thirty-seven. It is said that Duncan Edwards, the young Manchester United star who was later killed in the Munich air crash, was so impressed that he actually patted Hagan on the back as he trotted back to the centre circle.

Three weeks later United played Charlton Athletic at the Valley, going down 1-3 to an Eddie Firmani hat-trick, but all the papers were full of praise for the quality of football served up by United and, in particular, Jimmy Hagan.

One report called Hagan 'the quiet genius' and said:

When you see Len Shackleton you understand why inside forward skill comes to full flower so rarely; when you see Hagan you wonder why all the others don't do it.

He de-glamourizes the job; the perfect butler, always there, always doing the right thing, seemingly serving generations of impetuous younger colleagues.

The following week, on 11 December, Sheffield United beat Bolton Wanderers 2-0 at Bramall Lane, but it should have been a cricket score according to some papers. Joe Shaw blotted out Nat Lofthouse and United's attack was inspired by the brilliance of Hagan.

New Year's Day 1955 saw an amazing match against Newcastle United that older fans still talk about. The Blades had to reshuffle the team at the last minute when Cross was unfit. Hawksworth moved into the centre and the young John Spencer was brought in to play on the left wing. Newcastle had Simpson in goal – one of the best keepers in the land at that time.

Anyone arriving late for the match missed the most amazing start, for Sheffield United were 4-0 up after just eight minutes, with goals from Ringstead, Hagan, Hawksworth and Spencer. Newcastle pulled a goal back after ninteen minutes, but Hagan scored his second just after the half-hour. The match finished 6-2, with John Spencer getting United's last goal. In the closing minutes both Hagan and Spencer came close to getting their hat-tricks.

The great England defender, Harry Johnston, writing in February 1955, said:

> Hagan is one of the greatest inside-forwards of my time. I believe he will go down in soccer history along with players like Raich Carter and Peter Docherty.
>
> Like Len Shackleton, Hagan is a box-of-tricks, although he hasn't Shack's clowning instinct. But in ball play, he is one of the masters. Because he is not tall you will often see him on the field urging his colleagues to keep the ball down; Hagan with the ball at his feet, is a difficult man to stop.
>
> He has a host of tricks – the old Alex James 'foot-stutter' over the ball, for instance, to make an opponent check stride and miss his tackle, or the body swerve to right or left – which usually succeed in tearing a defence wide open.

Harry Johnston was well qualified to write about Hagan's skill for he had observed it at close quarters as one of the members of the England FA party that toured Canada in 1950.

For Jimmy, however, it was becoming harder to stay fully fit and injury-free, and again he missed a third of the season. His tally at the end was nine goals in 31 appearances in all competitions but Sheffield United finished in a respectable thirteenth place. Sheffield Wednesday, to the satisfaction of the red and white half of the city, finished bottom of the League and were relegated.

A sad footnote was the tragic loss of the much-respected manager, Reg Freeman, who was taken ill late in the season with cancer and died during the summer.

By the 1954/55 season football in general was changing and new commercial opportunities were being explored. Clubs were installing floodlights and playing night-time friendly matches against overseas teams, although it took a little longer for floodlit football to be approved for League matches. The improved lighting made televising matches much more of a practical proposition, particularly in winter.

It also brought in the phenomenon of 'All-Star' teams who played regularly up and down the country, and Jimmy was in demand for such games – so much so that the matter was raised in a board meeting. Some members were critical that Hagan was playing in friendly matches almost every week, but it seems they did not try to stop these extra-curricular activities which brought additional income for the players involved.

Other teams recognised that Hagan still had much to offer and in February 1955 Barrow approached the SUFC Board for permission to offer Hagan the position of player-coach. This was refused.

That Jimmy Hagan was a multi-faceted person is not in doubt. As well as being a professional footballer, sports outfitter and occasional journalist, he could also turn his hand to design.

The current Sheffield United logo, with crossed scimitars beneath a white rose, was officially adopted by the club for the 1977/78 season. However, this was actually largely designed by Jimmy Hagan in the early 1950s as a blazer badge for one of the club's end-of-season overseas tours. Jimmy's version had the letters 'SUFC' under the swords and the logo was enclosed within a traditional shield shape. The later version, adopted in 1977, had the same crossed swords and white rose, but surrounded by a red circle containing the words 'SHEFFIELD UNITED FC 1889'. The facts about Hagan's involvement in the design did not surface until after his death, but have been confirmed by both his children and other former friends of Jimmy. One wonders how he would have responded to the current Captain Blade pirate mascot, with his two scimitars. No doubt the mascot would have greatly appealed to his sense of humour and liking for fancy dress.

Through his sports outfitters' business Hagan regularly supplied ties and blazer badges to Sheffield United in the mid-1950s. This was with the express agreement of the board (with the proviso that it must not be to the detriment of the club's long-standing supplier, Jack Archer). It would appear that the board was happy to pass a little extra business to Hagan and Brook, for these were still the days of the Football League maximum wage.

One of Jimmy's unusual attributes was that he was completely ambidextrous. Not only could he kick and control a football equally well with either foot, he could play cricket and golf right or left-handed.

On the golf course he preferred to play left-handed, and he accordingly had a set of left-handed clubs. On one occasion, however, he was unexpectedly invited to play golf and the only clubs that he could borrow were a right-handed set. Undaunted, he played the eighteen holes right-handed, and still produced a score that most amateur golfers would be proud of!

.

CHAPTER TWELVE

The Twilight Years

Faced with finding a new manager at short notice, the board made a bold move by bringing in a 'big name' – Joe Mercer. At the same time the admission prices for all parts of the ground were raised significantly which led to the feeling amongst some fans – probably unjustifiably – that this was to help pay Mercer's salary. His playing credentials were second to none but he had never managed a club before, and he met the players for the first time on the eve of the first match of the season.

In fact, Mercer had no need to go into football management at all since he had a sizeable interest in a family grocery business in Hoylake. His long and impressive career as a player had come to an end with a broken leg at Highbury in the spring of 1954 when he was approaching forty. He had seldom been the kind of player who made the headlines, but always gave 100 per cent and was a natural leader. He had captained England and had played in 27 internationals.

To Jimmy Hagan, of course, Mercer was no stranger, for they both had been in the Army PT Corps at Aldershot and had played many matches together during the war. Jimmy greeted Mercer's arrival by popping his head round the manager's door and, with a twinkle in his eye, saying, 'Hello boss!'

Mercer had to learn the art of management quickly when faced with a spate of lengthy injuries to key players, including Hagan, and the team struggled for much of the season, eventually being relegated, although just two more points would have seen them safe. A decent cup run saw the team reach the fifth round before being beaten by Sunderland in a replay. Hagan played 27 games in all competitions and scored nine goals. As United were relegated, so Wednesday were promoted. The Sheffield see-saw continued.

By the beginning of 1956 it seems the board did not know what to do with Hagan. A coaching role was discussed, yet again, but Mercer told the board, 'Hagan has no future other than as a player on dry ground', and they considered parting with him at the end of the season. On 12 January they agreed to sell him to Rotherham United if they received a suitable offer, but this was not forthcoming. Just two weeks later they seem to have changed their minds. Following an approach from Nottingham Forest it was agreed to say 'nothing doing' to all enquiries for Hagan's services.

Joe Mercer was not popular with Blades fans and he came under stinging criticism the following season (1956/57) when he dropped Joe Shaw after nine games (which had brought five wins and two draws) and brought in a more traditional big central defender in Malcolm Barrass, rubbing salt into the wounds by immediately making him captain. At first, results did not suffer, but from the beginning of December the rot set in, with several heavy defeats. Barrass' best days were behind him and he was off the pace. After nearly four months (following a 1-5 defeat) Joe Shaw was restored to what virtually everyone regarded was his rightful place at centre half in January when Mercer had to concede that he had been wrong.

It wasn't just the fans who were critical of Mercer, for some of the board members wanted him out, but he rode the storm and received the dreaded 'Vote of Confidence' which, in his case, was honoured.

The team failed to fire on all cylinders consistently during the 1956/57 season and finished in seventh place with 46 points, eight points short of promotion. Mercer, who was struggling with team selection nearly every week, certainly needed Hagan's experience on the field. The maestro, now thirty-eight, could still amaze people, as seen in a 4-1 away win over Huddersfield Town on 3 November 1956. The journalist Dave Pardon reported:

> Four minutes after kick-off (the Huddersfield centre-half) Ken Quested's face bore a puzzled, baffled look as, with three of his colleagues, he was beaten by the greatest piece of ball-play I have seen.
>
> Jimmy Hagan beat four successive tackles without moving the ball outside a two-foot radius, put a gentle 30-yard crossfield pass to Waldock, and stood applauding Howitt's volleyed goal.
>
> Hagan was on form. He went through the first half with a fantastic display – an exhibition which put the crowd on his side, and cheering every time he put boot to ball. That was often enough to turn the Huddersfield defence into a shambles.

On 25 November 1956 Jimmy had something to celebrate when he became a father for the second time when his second child, a daughter – Jacqueline ('Jackie') – was born.

Hagan had a spell out injured from mid-January to the beginning of April but managed 27 League appearances, scoring seven goals. He produced yet another great performance on 13 April 1957 when Liverpool came to the Lane, desperately seeking points for promotion. Hagan was magnificent and destroyed them in a master class that tore the Liverpool team apart. United won 3-0 and the crowd rose to applaud Hagan as he left the field.

During the 1956/57 season Hagan also turned out on 1 October 1956 in a benefit match for Len Browning, whose promising career had been so cruelly cut short through illness. A combined Sheffield United/Wednesday XI beat a Leeds XI comprehensively 7-1, with Hagan scoring one of the goals, and 17,337 fans from both sides of the city joined forces on a Monday evening in a rare display of Sheffield togetherness.

As the 1957/58 season dawned, Hagan was approaching his fortieth year and Mercer informed him that he would not now be using him on a regular basis. When news of this reached the fans (many of whom seemed to believe that Hagan could go on for ever) it was another black mark against the unpopular manager. Mercer later wrote that Hagan took the news in his usual quiet, dignified way, and replied 'I'll be here if you need me'.

Despite rumours of a feud between the two, Hagan, in fact, had a lot of respect for Mercer, dating from their Army days when perhaps Mercer had helped to further Hagan's wartime international career. It is unlikely that Mercer, who was some four years older than Hagan, ever asked for advice from the Blades' hero (particularly in view of his comment to the board in January 1956: 'Hagan has no future other than as a player on dry ground'). Perhaps Mercer felt that if Hagan was given a coaching role he would undermine the manager, for Jimmy's stubbornness and desire to do things his way was legendary.

What is certain, however, is that Hagan never criticised the manager – publicly or privately – and they remained on good terms for many years.

Mercer had to face a perennial problem which has beset so many Sheffield United managers over the years – a lack of funds. He knew he had to rebuild the team, but to raise money he controversially sold one of the star players – Colin Grainger – to Sunderland and later the wing half, Jim Iley, to Spurs (curiously, Hagan had never rated Iley very highly). These, and other transfers, netted £65,000. He concentrated mainly on developing the young players who were already with the club, but he did eventually make one major signing: the striker Derek 'Doc' Pace from Aston Villa, who became a favourite with the Bramall Lane crowds.

By this time Jimmy Hagan and Stanley Matthews (three years his senior) were the last two footballers of the pre-war era still playing in the Football League. The modest Hagan's standing in the game was still high and he was touted in some quarters (and not just in Sheffield) for the Footballer of the Year award, although it ultimately went to Tom Finney.

As things turned out, Hagan played just four senior games at the start of the 1957/58 season, two at inside right, one on the left wing and one (surprisingly) at centre forward, but he did also play occasionally in the reserves. Mercer struggled to find a settled forward line during the first half of the season and it was not until he signed Derek Pace in December that he was able to put the final jigsaw pieces together. Pace banged in 22 goals from 26 matches.

The team finished in sixth place. Hagan's last first-team match was an away fixture against Derby County on 14 September 1957 when he was thirty-nine years and 236 days old. Coincidentally this was against the team that had sold him to Sheffield United some nineteen years earlier.

At a board meeting in October 1957 three directors commented that Hagan was 'too slow and should not play in either the first or second team, or in Tuesday practice matches'. They also expressed the view that Hagan should not be allowed to coach as he 'cannot impart his knowledge to the players'. This was an odd statement in view of his successful managerial career which followed, but it demonstrated that Hagan had made little effort to cultivate board members over the years and perhaps his relationship with many of the players was somewhat distant. Winning friends was never high in his priorities.

As Jimmy's playing career drew towards its end, he also suffered a blow in his family life when his mother, Catherine, died on 10 October 1957 at the age of sixty. His father, Alf Hagan, lived on until the mid-1970s and was thus able to share all the best moments of his son's career in football.

Jimmy the footballer was not finished, however, for he continued to turn out in various friendly matches and in 'All-Star Elevens', one being at Corby Town when they launched their new floodlights in February 1958. Hagan did not disappoint and scored two of his side's three goals. Hagan also scored for another All-Star XI during the season, this time at Newport County, when they switched on their floodlights.

The journalist Frank Butler wrote around this time:

Jimmy is retiring officially at the end of this season in the same mood as he started – without a grouse and without a regret. 'When I was a 14-year-old at Liverpool I aimed to play until I was 40,' he told me. 'If I had my life over again I'd still choose professional football.'

Jimmy's appearances in 'All-Star' teams continued for several years and took him all over the UK and sometimes to Ireland. Since football was played in Ireland on a Sunday the 'mercenaries' (who included Stanley Matthews) would catch the night boat from Liverpool on a Saturday evening to cross the Irish Sea, arriving in good time to play on a Sunday afternoon. On one occasion a poster advertising a match referred to 'Jimmy O'Hagan', presumably in error, but it was not far off the mark, considering his family's history.

There was one last hurrah for Hagan at Bramall Lane – a testimonial match on 10 March 1958. The board had begun discussing this six months earlier since sanction had to be given by the Football League. The ground was packed when 29,166 fans turned out on a very cold night, with snow on the pitch, to salute their hero – a much higher attendance than at any of the League games that season.

Such was the stature of Hagan in the game that he was able to attract a high-quality International XI to play against a combined Sheffield XI. Hagan turned out for the Internationals, who included such stars as Stanley Matthews, Brian Clough, Tom Finney, Jimmy McIlroy, Danny Blanchflower and Jimmy Armfield.

The weather was so bad that some of the star players could justifiably have pulled out of the game, but nobody did. Jimmy Armfield wrote in his autobiography that he and Tom Finney travelled across the Pennines in Stanley Matthews' car. Matthews was a notoriously bad driver – often taking his eyes off the road to turn and talk to his passengers – and they faced ice and snow on the return journey over the Woodhead Pass (the M62 had not yet been built). Tom Finney was mightily relieved when Matthews dropped him off, safe and sound, in Preston in the early hours. Jimmy Armfield was equally delighted when he reached his home in Blackpool unscathed. (Armfield's verdict on Jimmy Hagan, incidentally: 'a great player').

The score was 4-3 to the internationals, but this was immaterial as the spectators were treated to a feast of football under the floodlights. The fans were able to sing their anthem 'Wonderful, Wonderful Jimmy Hagan' one last time and tears were shed by many as Hagan saluted the crowd and trudged off the field at the end of the game.

Hagan wrote in the programme:

It is not easy to say 'Good-bye' in the game I have always loved and enjoyed but it will be readily understood that, at 40, the spirit is willing but the flesh is weak. The lucky breaks of the game have come my way and serious injury has passed me by. I have much to feel thankful about… My 20 years' association with Sheffield United have been very happy indeed. Where else could I have had better treatment from a management or more unselfish help from my colleagues on the field? To them I owe whatever success I have had. We have had the usual ups and downs associated with any club. I have been dropped a few times, too, but this only made me keener to regain my place.

Joe Mercer wrote:

Jimmy is a personality and an individual of the Stan Matthews, Raich Carter, Alex James and Dixie Dean status, who had the courage and confidence when facing any opposition to play his own, natural game.

In this modern, coaching conscious age, where we are all apt to sacrifice the individual on the altar of team tactics we may never see his like again. On his day, Jimmy was unplayable, but I think of all his many outstanding skills where he really excelled was his ability to bring a ball out of the air absolutely under control. I've heard half-backs complain 'It's a claw he's got – not a right foot.'

As a spontaneous wit he had few equals. And the grimmer the situation the more keen it became. With all his skill and apparently happy, carefree approach to the game, Jimmy has always been a fanatical trainer, a strict tee-totaller and non-smoker who has lived for his football. Jimmy trains himself and always has done, but what a hard taskmaster he has been. I've never known him not want to play, whether it has been a practice game, in the first team or reserve side, and I am confident there is not a player in England who has played in more benefit games than Jimmy.

Even when he has been dropped he has never uttered a word of complaint. His technique was to go into the reserve team and play so well that the embarrassment was reversed.

Jimmy's sense of humour was evident to the last. When the *Sheffield Telegraph* journalist Monty Marsden referred to the great support that he had received from spectators at the Lane over the years, Hagan replied: 'They used to shout "well played Jimmy". They also used to say "get off home Hagan". Well now, at last, I'm going.'

Hagan's playing statistics for Sheffield United are:

	Appearances	Goals
League	361	117
FA Cup	28	5
Total	389	122

He also scored 11 goals from 15 Sheffield County Cup appearances. If the war had not intervened he would clearly have played many more games for United, and almost certainly earned many full England caps, too.

Sheffield journalist Fred Walters wrote:

He will go down in my memory as one of the quickest thinking players I have ever known and that, as much as his ball control, has been the secret of his success.

Frank Taylor, writing in a national newspaper, said:

> If you want to know the most complete inside forward I have seen in post-war football – yes, you can include Puskas if you like – my vote would go to Jimmy Hagan. He was the cleverest with the ball and an accurate passer and finisher. For me, the tops.

Frank Swift, the former England goalkeeper, wrote:

> The record books make a mockery of his ability. To my mind, Jimmy was born 10 years too early. It is fantastic that the Sheffield wonder-man should be retiring from the game without having played in a full international against any of the home countries.
>
> But that has been Hagan's fate – odd man out in a golden era of England inside-forwards such as Raich Carter, Wilf Mannion and Len Shackleton.

Johnny Haynes, the Fulham and England star, wrote:

> Since I came into Fulham's team on Boxing Day 1952, I have paid a lot of attention to the style of opposing inside forwards.
>
> Jimmy Hagan, the Sheffield United veteran, is the best of them all, in my opinion. He has been the complete inside forward – goal-maker, goal-taker, attacking 'general', defensive-helper, and a good type on and off the field.
>
> It is soccer's loss that Hagan is retiring at the end of the season because personalities of his calibre are too few... long after he has retired he will remain in my memory as one of the great inside forward artists.

Walter Winterbottom also sent in this tribute:

> Jimmy Hagan was one of the cleverest inside forwards of his day. Many would say that he was unfortunate to gain only one international cap

against Denmark in 1949 for at that time Carter and Mannion were holding the inside forward positions for England.

Whenever Jimmy played one felt certain that he would bring some touch of his genius to highlight the game.

Those of us who know Jimmy well, know of his great sense of humour and in his play we could always see some humoured delight when he tricked his opponent by some quick thinking tactic or some deft use of his skill.

Jimmy has qualified as an FA coach and has helped as a member of staff at national courses at Lilleshall.

Here he is proving what we all expected, that he has still much to give to the game, and I hope he will serve it for many years to come.

The testimonial game was not Hagan's last appearance for the Blades, however. Just five days later he turned out for the Sheffield United reserves, helping them to a 4-4 draw against West Bromwich Albion reserves in front of a 2,600 crowd. As always, Hagan would never turn down the opportunity to play in a game of football. United were trailing 3-4 with a few minutes to go, but then, as the *Sheffield Telegraph* reported, 'Hagan controlled the ball, shrugged past Hughes, and beat Brown with a great shot that brought the goal of the match.'

A final word on the Joe Mercer chapter. As the 1958/59 season progressed the team started to perform better and produce results. But just as Mercer was beginning to win over his critics, he abruptly resigned at Christmas to take up the vacant manager's job at Aston Villa. Once again, he became the villain in the eyes of Unitedites.

CHAPTER THIRTEEN

Going Posh

As Hagan's thoughts turned to his future, when the season ended he was invited by Stanley Matthews (who rated Hagan as 'one of the best inside forwards of his day') to tour Australia with Blackpool as a guest player. Typically, Jimmy did not go just to make up the numbers and have a good time. He took every game seriously.

On their way to Australia, Blackpool had a match in Hong Kong against a Combined Chinese side. Expecting a tough match, the Chinese had picked their strongest team, and had worked out a strategy to keep Matthews quiet by putting two defenders permanently on the great man.

Hagan realised immediately what was going on and took over the mantle of schemer and playmaker. With the defenders concentrating on Matthews he took charge and, in a dazzling display of vintage Hagan, scored three goals in four minutes.

The Chinese team never recovered and Hagan went on to score six goals in a 10-0 victory. And this from a forty-year-old whose playing career was supposed to be finished!

Once in Australia, Hagan played in all five of Blackpool's matches during May 1958 and had a great tour, scoring six (possibly seven – the records are a little unclear) goals in one game alone. Although Matthews surely did not invite him for his goal-scoring ability, Hagan ended up as the highest scorer in the team with 28 goals.

As Hagan contemplated a future outside football – his sports out-fitters' venture continued successfully with himself as sole owner after Harold Brook was transferred to Leeds – it was obvious to others that his was far too great a talent to be lost to the game.

He had been approached from as early as 1952 by various clubs, offering him a player-manager's role, and the offers increased during his final year at Sheffield United, but he made it clear that his days as a footballer were over.

Clearly, Hagan had a good business brain but whether he intended to go into football management is uncertain. One thing was sure however: he would not rush into anything without careful consideration but, having done so, he would give it 100 per cent to ensure that he did the best possible job. By the same token, he would not accept any job if he felt it was not right for him.

He was interested, however, when Peterborough United – then a Midland League side – invited him to an interview for the manager's post after the departure of George Swindin. Another goalkeeper-manager had seemed likely when Ted Ditchburn was initially named as his successor, but after the directors had interviewed George Raynor and Jimmy Hagan in August 1958, Hagan got the job.

Jimmy arrived in Peterborough with his family, determined to make a success of his first managerial post. Although he had said that he would not be a player-manager, paradoxically, one of the first games at Peterborough happened to be a friendly match against the visiting South African national team. He was persuaded to play and, of course, stole the show. One wag wrote to the local newspaper suggesting that with performances like that he could play until he was eighty, as his economy of effort and total control of the game made fans realise the difference between Midland League and England quality.

The departing manager, ex-Arsenal goalkeeper George Swindin, had returned to Arsenal to be manager but had left the club in extremely good order. Jimmy settled into the job very easily, mainly because he had an excellent relationship with chairman Frank Stimpson and vice chairman Cyril Palmer. There was only one expectation at Peterborough and that was straightforward – entry into the Fourth Division of the Football League! They had been champions of the Midland League (in those days considered along with the Southern League as one of the best outside the Football League) for the past three years but had failed to get into the League because of the 'old boys' club'. The team finishing last in the Football League had to apply to all the other clubs for re-election to remain in the League. The chairmen had a cosy relationship with each other and usually voted the bottom club back in again.

Paul Mowforth, in *Never So Posh*, wrote of Hagan's arrival:

> Quietly, cautiously, a little apprehensively, Jimmy Hagan took over the reins at London Road. Everything was ready for the start of another record season and, sensible man that he is, Hagan let things run on the wheels which Swindin had already oiled… Mr Hagan approached the task with quiet confidence and was soon guiding the United to another championship and another memorable cup run.

Every year the supporters' club produced a yearbook for Peterborough United and Jimmy wrote a message for the 1959 edition that showed his candid but ambitious approach to his job:

> In the few months that I have been with Peterborough United I have been endeavouring to find my way, for there was much that I had to learn about the Club, how it was run in the past, and what plans it had for the future.
>
> The Board of Directors are very fair, hard working and devoting much of their valuable time to the success and well-being of the Club.
>
> I have also found that the Supporters' Club and its members are working enthusiastically and unselfishly to make Peterborough a great Club.
>
> Of the ground? Although not completed, it is the envy of many League Clubs. Now to the main asset 'the players'. I already knew

that the United were a good team, having watched and played against them. They play good football, and have some clever and talented players.

So far this season (up to the time of writing) they are unbeaten, winning most of their games fairly easily. Not a set-up which calls for drastic changes, as far as the Midland League side is concerned, but I am afraid that the Reserve Team picture is not so bright, as very few are up to Midland League standard.

Now to our aims? To win the Midland League for the fourth consecutive time, to have a successful run in the FA Cup, and then to realise a Peterborough dream by gaining admission to the Football League, as I am sure that no other Club has deserved this honour more than the 'Posh'.

We hear that present-day soccer needs new ideas and new blood. If that is so, then our Club should be welcomed with open arms; then it would be the duty of all concerned, the Management, the Players and the Supporters, to work together as a team, to consolidate our position in the League, to mould a solid foundation on which to build a Club that Peterborough can be proud of.

As I have stated, we have a good football side. It is not perfect, no team ever is, but in my opinion it is the best available, and good enough to win the Midland League again.

Now election to the Football League will bring with it many problems. As in the past, being a Non-League Club we were able to sign talented players from League Clubs who had a fee placed upon them, and we were free to do so, but once we obtain League status, to acquire these players (and we have a few now) we should have to pay the Transfer Fee demanded.

Yes, our Team needs strengthening for a higher class of football, and as our finances are low, and Transfer Fees are high, we shall have to develop our players from this area. They shall be encouraged, coached and given every chance to improve their soccer. We want them to be really proud to wear the Royal Blue Jerseys of Peterborough United, but how I wish that we had a suitable practice pitch for these lads.

In brief, that is an outline of our aims. To carry them through we need the loyal support of all Peterborough sportsmen, and we need it more than ever when things are not just going right, and believe me, football is such an unpredictable game, one day you are up, and the next you could be down. Therefore, if any individual player is having a bad time; he knows it better than anyone. Give him encouragement.

Encouragement works wonders, on some grounds it is worth a goal start. We have had experience at Sheffield, Liverpool, Everton, Hampden Park and other places, so let us have more of the London Road Roar; that is your job. We can't make it without your support, a strong Club shall be an asset to this City, and if we all pull together we can make Peterborough United a great Club.

Peterborough duly won the Midland League for the fourth year in a row, in a canter as usual, but their application to join the Football League was denied yet again, even though Jimmy called in debts from his playing colleagues at other clubs.

In the 1959/60 season, he set about trying to canvass clubs with brochures and invitations to Peterborough to see their facilities, which were far better than most Fourth Division clubs at that time. The manager and chairman both realised that this could be their year, if the club applying for re-election were suitable candidates to be replaced. Fate decreed that Gateshead (ironically, the closest League club to Jimmy's birthplace) finished bottom of the League in 1960/61 and because of the fact that they were an isolated club (in the far north-east of the country) and had poor gates, and Peterborough had done their canvassing well, Peterborough won the Midland League for the fifth season in a row and were duly elected to the Football League. Jimmy Hagan thus became a League manager.

The fact that the Posh had average gates of over 10,000 as a non-League club gave expectations of even better in the Fourth Division and people were not disappointed.

A new grandstand and floodlighting system were installed to coincide with their arrival in the Football League and the club got off to a great start with a capacity of 20,000 for their first game at home to Wrexham

Posh went on to set a new standard for a League club with a record points total and a record goals total (134) in their very first year. They also had the top goalscorer in Terry Bly with 52 goals (still a record). Up they went into the Third Division, along with their closest rivals, Crystal Palace.

The sports editor of the *Peterborough Standard* wrote:

> Peterborough United have shaken the soccer world with their brilliant record-breaking debut in League Football, and while the whole city basks in the reflected glory of the honours won by Posh I would like to add a personal tribute and say, quite sincerely, United you astounded us all.
>
> Astounded? Yes… For a club to achieve so much in its first season in League football is amazing. Personally I didn't think it possible, and I don't for one moment ever expect to see the same thing happen again.
>
> Only a team of the calibre of Posh could have pulled it off so calmly and with such assurance.
>
> Five times Midland League champions, winners of all the non-League glory for many seasons, United were tailor-made for success, but it took a craftsman like Manager Jimmy Hagan and a lot of hard graft to put the club where it is today.

The team in that memorable year was built around a relatively small squad of players. The goalkeeper, Jack Walls, had his best season since joining the club; right-back Dick Whittaker took his chance when Ellis Stafford injured an ankle and kept the shirt for the rest of the season; left-back Jim Walker was one of the best defenders in the League; Jim Rayner, switched from centre forward to right half-back by Hagan, was a revelation; centre half and captain, big Norman Rigby, had kept his place despite being a part-time player; left half-back Keith Ripley steadily improved over the season to become a powerhouse in the side; Peter McNamee and Billy Hails were wingers in the old fashioned sense who could beat their full back and also score goals (right-winger Billy Hails had a great season, scoring 24); inside forward Denis Emery, a part-timer, was a master of positional play (Denis was an elegant inside forward who Jimmy admired for his ability to effortlessly round goalkeepers on one-on-one situations, and once said how he wished Denis could teach some internationals how to dribble around the goalkeeper); Terry Bly, centre forward, had been rescued by Hagan from Norwich City where, it was said, he had lost his goal touch, scored a remarkable 54 goals in the season – not far off Dixie Dean's record of 60; inside left Ray Smith completed the forward line. The trainer, John Anderson, was extremely popular with the players and a very able right-hand man for the manager.

Terry Bly's season had been so remarkable that Peterborough could not hold on to him and he was sold to Coventry City. Hagan replaced him with another astute buy, George Hudson. He had played at London Road for Accrington Stanley a month before the club went bankrupt. He scored a hat-trick in a 4-3 defeat and as soon as the pending bankruptcy became public, Jimmy was to head north and snap up Hudson for a song (Hudson, like Bly, would also be sold later to Coventry for a fee in excess of £30,000). This was to become another trademark of Jimmy's managerial career: the ability to spot talent at a good price.

Jimmy had developed a team which could hold its own with some of the best. This was proven in the numerous scalps that were claimed in the FA Cup runs for which the Posh had become famous. Trips to Walsall, Ipswich, Portsmouth and Newcastle all produced wins. Memorable ties resulting in replays with Fulham and Aston Villa (attendance 64,531) added to the reputation of Peterborough United.

The cup game at St James' Park produced a problem of a different kind for Jimmy. The Newcastle chairman at that time was Stan Seymour, who had played in the same Newcastle side as Alfie Hagan some forty years earlier. Seymour invited Alfie to the director's boardroom after the match, along with Jimmy, for a few drinks (non-alcoholic in Jimmy's case, of course). Alfie enjoyed the hospitality rather too well and started making pointed remarks about Peterborough's win over the mighty Newcastle, which ruffled a few feathers. Fortunately David Hagan was waiting for his dad outside, and Jimmy got his son to escort Alfie home in a taxi.

Jimmy had a team which he later rated among the best he ever had in terms of playing an attacking brand of football and he gave them their head on the field to play with a swashbuckling style (best of seven goals was almost commonplace!) Off the field, however, although he was not unfriendly, he did not mix with the players a great deal and he ruled with discipline and a hand of steel. This did not go down well with some of the team. This trait, and a stubborn sense of ethics, was prevalent in all his future managerial positions. On one occasion at Peterborough no fewer than seven players demanded to be put on the transfer list!

As manager of Peterborough's successful football team Jimmy Hagan found himself part of the local establishment and he and Iris were often invited to attend – and sometime 'perform' at – public functions. Although Jimmy was essentially a private man and hated to be in the limelight, he and Iris carried out their public duties impeccably, turning out at mayoral receptions, fetes, and the like.

If Jimmy thought an issue was right and proper in his eyes he could be totally uncompromising. After the departure of Frank Stimson and Cyril Palmer – chairmen at Peterborough United for whom he had the utmost respect – came a retired sub-postmaster called Tommy Peake. The promotion of Peake to the chair of the club was to be the beginning of the end for Jimmy who virtually refused to discuss football matters with someone who 'knew so little about the game'. This echoes the thoughts of his old friend Len Shackleton and the chapter in his book about the average director and his knowledge of football – the chapter was left blank!

Jimmy had broken many records at Peterborough and had thoroughly enjoyed the practical side of coaching the team, and the success that it brought in his first foray into management. He did not, however, enjoy some of the boardroom politics and the relentless media attention. After refusing to back down on issues relating to football and input from the chairman, he was asked to resign. He refused, and was sacked.

He left Peterborough United in October 1962 when the club was lying second in the old Third Division, a position that proved to be the high point in the club's history and one that they have never again achieved. Hagan left the club in a most healthy position with a mixture of experienced and young players who were purchased for next to nothing or on free transfers. He most certainly had an eye for players who could bring something to a club for little outlay. Among these were Keith Ripley, bought from Leeds, who had a reputation as a hellraiser but was one of the key players in the promotion from the old Fourth Division; Terry Bly and George Hudson, mentioned before, as strikers who had a real eye for goal and who made a lot of money for Peterborough after selling them on; Terry Simpson, who he bought from Southampton, was brought in as a midfielder and covered every inch of the pitch with real pace; Ollie Hopkins, an old-fashioned centre half from Barnsley; and Tommy Singleton, a stylish full-back from Blackpool. These signings, along with the established players, made Peterborough a team who were genuinely feared.

The Posh had a wonderful away following and large attendances at home which they can only dream about today. One of the games which Jimmy enjoyed the most was a clash with his old club, Sheffield United. The FA Cup game attracted 28,174 to London Road and Posh were flying high after beating Colchester United after a second-replay victory at neutral Carrow Road. There was to be no fairy-tale end for Peterborough this year, however, as the Blades ran out 3-1 winners after scoring three goals in twenty minutes. When they were still a non-league team, Jimmy took Peterborough to Hillsborough in 1959/60. After giving as good as they got, and holding out for seventy-five minutes (and also having a disputed penalty appeal turned down), the game ended 2-0 to Wednesday – 51,144 spectators had witnessed a great game of football.

He departed Peterborough having been the most successful manager in the club's history (even up to the present day, his record is far superior to that of any other manager).

His sacking made national headlines since it was so unusual for a club at the peak of its success to get rid of their manager. Roy Ullyett, sports cartoonist for the *Daily Express*, even marked the occasion with a cartoon as a salutary warning to all managers of clubs in less successful positions!

Jim Walker, who played in Hagan's championship-winning side, remarked some years later, 'Jimmy was a terrific football manager, dedicated to bringing success to Posh. He was also a lovely chap off the field.'

Perhaps aided by more than £4,000 compensation he received from Peterborough, Hagan did not rush back into football management. Instead he spent some of his time writing a book about football boardroom intrigue. Sadly it was never finished and so never saw the light of day, but it would have been fascinating to learn of his views at the time.

For Jimmy's long-suffering wife, Iris, the first foray into football management had not made her enigmatic husband any easier to live with than when he was a player; quite the opposite, in fact, for he had treated the job with typical single-mindedness. Iris remarked to Hagan's accountant, Don Ward (who first looked after his tax affairs when he managed Peterborough and remained a good friend for the next thirty years), 'I've been married to Jimmy for more than twenty years, and I still don't know him!'

CHAPTER FOURTEEN

West Bromwich Albion

After his successes with Peterborough United, and the attacking style of football that Peterborough had played, it was clear that he would not be out of the game for very long, but he waited for six months until the right job came along. That opportunity came at a club in the First Division with a wonderfully rich tradition in the game – West Bromwich Albion – and he was appointed manager in April 1963.

From the time he left Peterborough he had kept himself in top physical shape, training every day. Even when there was snow and ice on the ground, he would drive his car into the country and put in a full training stint. 'I simply had to keep fit,' he said, and this meant that when he took over at West Bromwich, he could lead by example. All his life, he had never smoked or drunk, and he also paid careful attention to his diet. He was a sparse eater and firmly believed that it was better to under-eat than over-eat. A typical day would start with toast and breakfast cereal. He would have nothing further to eat until his evening meal around 7p.m.

West Bromwich Albion had been very successful in the 1950s, playing an attractive, imaginative and stylish brand of attacking football under Vic Buckingham, but their efforts had never quite earned them a trophy since their FA Cup success in the early fifties.

After Buckingham's departure to Ajax in 1959, the club went into a decline, and Jimmy Hagan was seen as the man to arrest the slide.

He was not impressed with the team that had been left to his guidance. He saw them as lightweight, slow and defensively minded. One of his first moves was to raid Peterborough and swap a centre forward, Keith Smith, with a player he had bought for Peterborough, Terry Simpson, who was athletic, quick and hard working. He also bought Ollie Hopkins, a no-nonsense centre-back.

His other steps were to sign the Scunthorpe United centre forward, John Kaye, who was to become a twin striker with Jeff Astle and terrorise defences and goalkeepers alike. Older Albion fans will recall a home game with Spurs and the unfortunate Bill Brown who conceded four goals which were literally headed out of his hands into the net. Kaye was a tough, hard-working player who became a firm favourite with Baggies fans. He was also good in the air.

Hagan also bought the then Queens Park Rangers' full-back, Bill Williams, who along with Kaye he had watched when managing the Posh. He was also to sign John Osborne who replaced Ray Potter in goal.

Bill Williams formed an all-Williams full-back duo with Graham Williams, who Jimmy really liked for his tough tackling, character and free-kick skills. Graham Williams was soon to become captain.

He tried to ensure that the team played entertaining football. 'The crowd pay to be entertained,' he said. 'They want football that lifts them out of their seats. This means goalmouth incidents. I deplore the growth of the defensive blanket, but to many clubs today, the result means everything.'

In September 1964 Hagan signed striker Jeff Astle from Notts County for £25,000. This has since been generally regarded as one of the best bits of transfer business in the club's history, for over the next decade Astle was to become the club's most iconic player ever. Hagan went to Notts County initially to watch Tony Hateley but became more and more impressed by Astle, who Jimmy thought had a far better all-round game than Hateley. He was, as ever, extremely careful when using the club's money and got his man, paying less than the initial asking price. This was a trait of Jimmy's at all his clubs. He seemed to know the true value of a player and would not pay over the odds. Alan Everiss, the club secretary, was to say about Jimmy that 'he treated our money as his own' and the club remained in good financial health.

While at WBA Jimmy tried to introduce young new players into the first team. He especially wanted players with skill, speed and an attacking nature. Among these were Tony Brown, who was to play for England, and Ian Collard, who he had huge hopes for, but never really made a name for himself. He also had Scottish internationals Bobby Hope and Doug Fraser, who were classy midfield players. Clive Clark was a very effective left-winger who Jimmy encouraged to steal in at the far post and score more goals.

The club was already feeling the dramatic social changes of the 1960s, tangibly through falling attendances and the end of the players' maximum wage restrictions. Hagan, perhaps not in tune with the swinging sixties, did not take easily to the players' new-found power and remained a martinet on the training ground – which frequently led to conflict with the playing squad.

In one of his fall-outs the players complained they found Hagan's training routines boring. On another occasion, on a cold December morning in 1963, the team captain, Don Howe, and other players refused to train unless they were allowed to wear tracksuit bottoms. Hagan, mindful of the fact that the team had to play their matches in shorts, said they could warm up in tracksuits but they had to train in shorts from the appointed time that training started. The team went on strike.

Peace was soon restored but Howe left the club a few months later. Typically, when the incident blew up, Hagan refused to make any public comment. Whatever he had to say was done in private. Don Howe, later in his career as Arsenal manager, admitted to Jimmy that he now saw things differently and that he would have done the same in his position as manager.

Jimmy did make his views on training clear in an interview with *The Weekly News* of 25 January 1964:

A player must be one hundred per cent fit. Ninety-nine per cent is just not good enough. The first essential today is stamina. A player must be able to withstand the tremendous pressure that can be put on him from time to time in a match. The next most important thing is quickness. Players must be alert, physically and mentally.

Most professional clubs at the time had two-hour training sessions. Jimmy, however, reduced his to ninety minutes but kept the players flat out for the whole period. Furthermore, he would never ask the players to do anything that he could not do himself, despite now being in his mid-forties. Not for nothing did he acquire the nickname 'The Iron Man'.

Not everything went to plan at Jimmy's training sessions, however. In January 1964, whilst reversing his Vauxhall Cresta car at the training ground, his foot slipped off the brake pedal. The car somersaulted four times down a steep 150-foot bank and landed – fortunately the right way up – in a canal. The car was a write-off. Hagan, with bruises and a cut head, crawled through the smashed windscreen and stood on the bonnet until five Albion players scrambled down the bank to help him.

Graham Williams and Terry Simpson reached Hagan first. 'We were amazed to find him so unruffled,' said Graham. Later, in hospital, his dry sense of humour came to the fore when he remarked, 'If the players move as quickly against Arsenal as they did to help me, then we shall be all right.'

Albion played Arsenal in the FA Cup fourth round the day after his accident. Don Howe, leader of the strike a few weeks earlier, but still the club skipper, sent a message to West Bromwich fans: 'We must win this one now. We can't let the boss down.' One can only assume that his feelings were genuine, which shows that he still had a lot of respect for his manager.

Throughout his managerial career in England Hagan found it almost impossible to relax. 'I guess that even when I'm away from the ground football problems are always running around my head. I simply live for football,' he confided.

Despite the battles with players, and sometimes the fans, Hagan shrewdly developed the team in personnel and skill, leading them to a League Cup triumph in 1966, and they finished that season in sixth place in the First Division.

In the last League Cup final to be played over two legs, against high-flying West Ham United, Albion were 1-2 down from the first leg at Upton Park. However, they put on a storming performance in the second leg to win 4-1 and thus take the tie 5-3 on aggregate. It all happened in the first half. Albion scored the first goal on nine minutes, and were four up after thirty-five minutes with goals from John Kaye, Tony Brown, Clive Clark and Graham Williams. The win earned West Bromwich Albion a place in Europe for the following season. The star-studded West Ham team that they defeated included such luminaries as Bobby Moore, Martin Peters, Geoff Hurst and Peter Brabrook.

After the match, the fans shouted repeatedly for Hagan and refused to disperse until the manager appeared to take the acclaim. Just a year earlier many of the same fans had been howling for his blood. Such is the fickleness of fans, and the lot of a football manager.

One national newspaper summed up the achievement:

Iron man Jimmy Hagan, inside-forward wizard of two decades ago, stalked proudly to the front rank of British managers as his non-stop Albion battlers thrashed West Ham. Thousands of frenzied supporters swarmed on to the pitch to watch the League Cup presented. The name 'Hagan' was chanted wildly – and track-suit rows and transfer disputes were things of the past.

It was a sweet triumph for those who, like Hagan, still believe that simple, old-fashioned Soccer can conquer new-fangled, modern defensive methods. Afterwards Hagan said: 'It's nice to have won something at last. That first goal was vital. It put us in with a chance, and I thought the boys did all I could have asked.'

For the record, the victorious team was: Potter, Cram, Fairfax, Fraser, Campbell, Williams, Brown, Astle, Kaye, Hope and Clark.

The following season was a hollow disappointment, with Albion losing in the final of the League Cup to Third Division Queens Park Rangers, who had also begun their relentless march towards First Division status with the Rodney Marsh era. Albion were 2-0 up at half-time, despite playing with a very inexperienced goalkeeper in Dick Shepherd. QPR managed to turn it around in the second half and won 3-2. The inquest after the game centred on whether Albion had decided to shut up shop in the second half. Bobby Cram, right full-back on the day, said that the tactics given at half-time cost them the game. However, the captain, Graham Williams, was to say later that Hagan simply asked for more of the same in the second half. When looking at Hagan's career, the latter seemed far more likely.

After an early exit from their first European campaign, against Bologna of Italy, and with Albion also struggling to maintain their place in the First Division, Jimmy's days were numbered. Had not the three setbacks happened in quick succession he might have been given time to fix the problems but in May 1967 he was replaced by Alan Ashman, who was to lead Albion to FA Cup victory in 1968, largely with the team that Hagan had assembled. Astle became the first player to score in every round.

Jimmy did leave a lot of friends at West Bromwich Albion, especially the back-room staff and directors who appreciated his integrity and dedication. Also a number of players, including Jeff Astle and Tony Brown, remained friends and always spoke very highly of him.

During his tenure as the West Brom manager, Hagan turned out to play at Bramall Lane again at the age of forty-seven in Joe Shaw's testimonial match on 29 March 1965. The crowds turned out to honour their other hero, Joe Shaw, but also to see the maestro again. Hagan, by now looking a little thinner than in his heyday, did not disappoint. Although he could not run around as much as he used to, once given the ball the years fell away and the old magic was still there for all to see and marvel at. Hagan was initially put down to play in an International XI, but when he arrived at the ground he insisted that he always regarded himself as a Sheffield United player and he demanded to be put in the 'home' team. A hasty reshuffle was made to accommodate him.

Now a top-flight manager and used to having his way, he was no longer the quiet man in the dressing room, and he set about instructing his much younger teammates on how he wanted them to play. 'I can't chase after the ball now, so I want it passed to my feet,' he told Mick Jones, later berating him when he failed to live up to his own exacting standards. Jones, then twenty, was a rising star on the verge of his first full England cap, and Hagan had been one of his boyhood heroes. He was surprised, and a little miffed, to be treated like a junior, but kept his peace out of respect for the man. Hagan probably had not intended to cause offence but he was never satisfied simply to turn out for a game. He always wanted to give of his best, and never more so than at Bramall Lane in front of his fans.

The *Star* journalist, Les Payne, who had never seen Hagan before that match, wrote many years later:

> I can remember nothing, not even Hagan's goal, apart from one moment of skill which combined awareness and wonderful passing. The ball came to Hagan in the centre circle. He was facing the other way but he controlled the ball, spun and played a pass which actually curled inside the right back and into the path of United left winger, Barry Hartle. It was an example of the highest skill. It was the hallmark of a great player. It was the moment I knew that every Hagan tale I'd been told just HAD to be right.

A month later Hagan turned out again at Stanley Matthews' testimonial night at Stoke City's ground. Matthews, being the legend that he was, had no fewer than two testimonial games in one evening and Hagan played in the preliminary match, billed as 'post-war favourites', between Harry Johnston's XI and Wally Barnes' XI. The two teams lined up: Bert Trautmann, Tim Ward, George Hardwick, Jimmy Hill, Neil Franklin, Harry Johnston, Don Revie, Stan Mortensen, Nat Lofthouse, Jimmy Hagan and Tom Finney, against Jimmy O'Neil, Jimmy Scoular,

Wally Barnes, Danny Blanchflower, Jimmy Dickinson, Hughie Kelly, Bill McGarry, Jackie Mudie, Jackie Milburn, Jock Dodds and Ken Barnes.

Matthews wrote in his book, *The Way it Was*:

> For the very last time people saw the sophisticated artistry of Tom Finney and Jimmy Hagan, the still lethal shooting of Morty, Jackie Milburn and Nat Lofthouse, the crunch tackling of Harry Johnston and Jimmy Scoular, the heading of Neil Franklin that mixed power, grace and style, and, the most blessed sight of all, burly Jock Dodds, one time Blackpool (and Sheffield United) and my old RAF pal, slower in pace but not in mind or reflexes, harnessing all and sundry, appealing for justice and, as of yore, getting very little.

It must have been a memorable spectacle for those fortunate to be present on that night. The main match featured current England stars in Stan's XI and an International XI of world-renowned players.

After leaving West Bromwich Albion Jimmy received a five-figure sum in compensation from the club so he had no need to rush back into the managerial job market. For a time he ran his own driving school, which he named 'No-eL Driving School'. Typically, he tackled the job properly, passing his advanced driving test and buying a dual-control car for the lessons. It is said that he enjoyed the experience and was probably glad to have a break from football management, which had twice kicked him in the teeth. He actually bought a second dual-control car as a back-up; this was another example of Hagan's thoroughness for he never employed any other instructors and ran the school single-handedly. He made a success of the business, although it is difficult to square the image of the strict disciplinarian, who was not easy to get to know, and who did not suffer fools gladly, having the patience to teach learner drivers to drive. However, he had taught physical training exercises to soldiers and was also an FA qualified coach, so perhaps teaching driving skills was not such a strange choice of career. Certainly many of his successful pupils spoke very highly of his patience and professionalism.

Hagan continued to be a valued member of the FA's coaching staff at Lilleshall, something he had combined with his work as a football manager for a number of years.

Another perk that he enjoyed was as a member of the Pools Panel, which would meet during bad weather to give their 'results' of any postponed matches. This involved a trip to London for the weekend, and five-star treatment at the Waldorf Hotel.

He was happily settled in the Birmingham area, living at 115 Walsall Road, Little Aston, in the same house that he had occupied as manager of West Bromwich Albion. When he parted company from the club the chairman, Bert Millichip, let Hagan buy the house at a favourable price – an indication that he was still held in some regard by the club.

Just around the corner were his good friends, Joe and Norah Mercer. His daughter, Jackie, recalls that the Mercers sometimes used to babysit when Jimmy and Iris wanted to have a night out. Joe Mercer was manager of Manchester City at this time and Jimmy did some scouting for the club, as well as others. As with everything he did, he was very professional and thorough, writing detailed reports which Iris typed out for him.

CHAPTER FIFTEEN

Benfica

During Hagan's time at West Bromwich England hosted the 1966 World Cup and Jimmy keenly watched many of the games. He shrewdly spotted the potential of Portugal very early in the series, and particularly of one of their players – Eusébio. Hagan was full of admiration for the twenty-four-year-old maestro (whom he always maintained was a better all-round player than Pele). Hagan was not surprised when Portugal finished third in the World Cup that year.

Eusébio had been the star of Benfica (or Sport Lisboa e Benfica to give the club its full name) since 1961. Benfica, founded as a multi-sports club in the early twentieth century, had been the dominant force in Portuguese football since the 1930s, winning the Portuguese national championship and cup on numerous occasions and reputedly having the support of over sixty per cent of the population of Portugal. In 1950 Benfica had won the Taca Latina, a forerunner of the Champions League, under an English coach, Edward 'Ted' Smith (formerly of Millwall), but it was during the 1960s that the club really dominated in Europe. Benfica won the European Cup in 1961 and 1962 and, although they were not to win a European trophy again, they reached the finals on several occasions. The team probably reached its peak in 1968 when it was generally regarded as the best in Europe.

By 1970, however, standards had begun to slip. Although Eusébio was still the star of the side it was felt that some of the other big-name players had become complacent and were not pulling their weight. The management was persuaded that an English coach was needed to restore some discipline and organisation in the side. It is said that Alf Ramsey had been approached but turned them down. He was still the England manager, after all.

The former Manchester United winger and Mansfield Town and Newcastle United manager, Charlie Mitten, who had some connections in Portugal, recommended that Jimmy Hagan was just the man to restore the club's fortunes. It was a far cry from the English Midlands but Jimmy was offered the job and decided to accept the challenge, although some eyebrows were raised back home.

Unlike the present day, when football managers (or coaches) of leading clubs can demand lucrative contracts that can virtually set them up for life, Jimmy was offered no perks – just a basic salary. He even had to rent his own house and buy his own car.

The management system of football clubs in Portugal (and in many other continental countries) is different from that of the UK. The coach was hired purely to train the side and look after matters on the field. He did not get involved in transfers of players (other than perhaps in an advisory capacity) or wage negotiations and the financial side of the club was looked after by a general manager under the control of the club president – often a powerful, political figure. Coaches had a high profile, too, but tended not to last long at Benfica. Many survived just a single season. Two years was average, and three was rare.

It seems odd that Hagan – very much his own man – even considered the position since his previous track record with club chairmen and directors had not always been happy. Perhaps during those long hours of teaching people to drive he had felt that his life was stagnating and that he was not likely to be offered another manager's job with a top British side. Or maybe he just fancied a new type of challenge in sunny Portugal. Hagan always thought deeply about things and did not make rash decisions, so one can assume that he considered all the angles and felt that he could make the challenge work. He did, however, insist on a number of clauses in his contract that gave him a high degree of control in on-field matters, including team selection.

Nevertheless, with his track record, and that of the Benfica club, it looked like an explosive confrontation waiting to happen.

He flew into Lisbon in February 1970, alone (Iris and Jackie followed a few weeks later), and with little or no knowledge of the Portuguese language. He was immediately made welcome and one of the Benfica players, Artur Jorge, initially acted as translator. After a while Jimmy mastered some basic words and phrases, including the necessary football speak, and could make himself understood with the players.

Against all the odds, Hagan got on well with the Benfica club president, Dr Duarte António Borges Coutinho. The two strong characters quickly developed a respect for each other, and Hagan was left to run the football team without any undue interference from the top. The 1969/70 season was drawing to a close and Benfica were not in their customary position at the top of the League. The team spirit was low and Jimmy quickly observed that many of the players were simply not fit. Laziness was something that he simply would not tolerate from players and he set about cracking the whip.

Hagan, who by now was over fifty, was still very fit and he often led the way in training, so players who were half his age could hardly complain. Jimmy could also still display his wonderful ball control and dazzling range of skills, so he soon earned the respect of the players. In Eusébio, Hagan recognised a kindred spirit and the two hit it off from the start. Both had come from humble working-class backgrounds and had displayed precocious talent as teenagers. Eusébio had been plucked from the relative obscurity of Portuguese East Africa (Mozambique) and brought to Benfica at the age of eighteen.

Eusébio later said of Hagan: 'Before his arrival, Portuguese players were not used to stringent physical preparation. Jimmy Hagan was a strong man and a good disciplinarian, but some players thought they were being pushed too hard. I can remember players being sick after some training sessions.'

Just one of Hagan's stamina-building training routines was to get the players to run up and down the steps of the grandstand of the famous Estádio da Luz. It was a killer, and perhaps similar to routines he had learnt during his Army days (the Estádio da Luz is often referred to in Britain as the Stadium of Light, but this is a misnomer – Luz is the name of the district where the ground is located).

After a while it dawned on the players what was happening. They were winning more games because they still had strength and fitness in the second half. This, along with their skilful play, was a major factor in their success under Hagan.

Hagan never spared himself in training, and when the normal session was over he would be happy to stay on and provide individual coaching to players. Even Eusébio benefited, and Hagan worked to improve his heading ability (which was ironic since Hagan, the player, seldom headed the ball!).

At the end of training one day he set all the players a test – to hit the crossbar from the edge of the penalty area. Jimmy showed them how to do it (this was a party piece of his and he could do it virtually every time). Then he showered, changed and had some lunch before returning to find a number of players still out there trying to do it!

As far as the fans – the 'Benfiquistas' – were concerned, Hagan was a hero. Being mobbed everywhere he went by excitable fans was something the modest and private man had to get used to, but he accepted it as part of the job. He was now universally known as 'Meeshter Haggan'.

He was not popular with the press, though, for he disliked giving interviews and would usually brush off any journalist with the words 'No comment'. This led to his being given the nickname 'Mister No Comment' by the media, or sometimes 'The Lone Wolf'. The local football media were much more demanding and confrontational at that time than Jimmy had been used to in England and he infuriated some journalists by not cooperating with them. Hagan let events on the field do his talking for him, and the football writers could hardly be too critical of him when the team was winning matches regularly.

There were many times however, when Hagan's other side would manifest itself, for he was capable of extreme acts of kindness. His former accountant, Don Ward, recalls:

He treated me wonderfully and I have only kind words to say about him. For instance, the phone rang one day and it was Jimmy. 'Are you doing anything next week?' he asked. I told him 'No' and he said 'Why don't you come out to Portugal and stay with us for a while? We've got a big game coming up.' This was typical of him. I flew out and was made most welcome by Jimmy and Iris. They wined and dined me, and I was taken to watch the big game as an honoured guest.

But one morning, when I was watching the players in training, I approached Eusébio for his autograph. Jimmy immediately intervened and said firmly, 'This is not allowed, Don. If you want Eusébio's autograph I'll get it for you later.' I felt like a schoolboy being told off by the headmaster, but I suppose he didn't take kindly to anyone interfering with his training sessions. He had to be in control.

Don Ward's summing up of Hagan is:

He was very deep – a loner. He didn't take to many people but could be very good company, and very generous, to those who were fortunate enough to be in his circle of friends. It seemed as though he chose people. I have no idea why he took to me. In all the years I knew him we never had any cross words.

Under Hagan's strict coaching the club achieved three successive League Championships (1971, 1972, 1973) and the Portuguese Cup (1972, beating their big rivals, Sporting Lisbon, 3-2). They were also runners-up in the cup in 1971.

Benfica is still the only Portuguese club to have gone through a whole season in the League without defeat, which they did under Hagan in 1972/73. They won 28 out of 30 matches (23 of them on the trot) and drew two away games (at FC Porto and Atlético). In the same season Eusébio won the European Golden Boot with 40 goals in what was his penultimate season as a Benfica player. The team scored 101 goals, breaking 100 for only the second time in their history. No other Portuguese club has even come close to this achievement.

The team also did well initially in the European Cup under Hagan. In the 1970/71 campaign they beat Feyenoord in the quarter-finals but were defeated by Ajax in the semi-final.

Despite having restored success to Benfica, there were tensions between Hagan and some of the players, a few of whom tried to undermine him. Matters came to a head on the occasion of Eusébio's testimonial match in September 1973. It was a prestigious occasion with international star guests, including Bobby Moore.

Hagan, like Eusébio, treated the testimonial as a serious match, and prepared the team accordingly. But whilst Eusébio trained normally, some players did not take the occasion seriously. Hagan warned them that if they didn't train properly he would not pick them for the game, but three players, Toni, Humberto and Diamantino, continued to laze around. As always, Hagan would not tolerate indiscipline and he told the three players that they would not be playing in the testimonial match.

Word of the dispute reached the Benfica club president, Borges Coutinho, before the game. Perhaps the pre-match socialising had clouded his judgment, for he had had a few drinks. He summoned Hagan and told him that the three dropped stars must play. Hagan pointed out that under the terms of his contract, he had full control over team selection, and refused. Coutinho thought he was bluffing and privately told Toni, Humberto and Diamantino that they would play.

When the players ran on to the field to warm up, and Hagan realised that he had been overruled, his reaction was immediate and decisive: he walked out of the club, never to return. He had been looking forward to the star-studded testimonial game as much as anyone, but that now took second place to a matter of principle.

A big reception for Eusébio had been arranged after the game at the casino, and Iris was getting herself ready for this when her husband arrived home, much earlier than expected, to drop the bombshell that he had quit his job. Iris was used to Jimmy's stubbornness and quirky behaviour, but this was totally unexpected. She did her best to reason with him but it was a forlorn hope. Jimmy's pride would not allow him to back down.

After the match there was a knock on the door and Jimmy was confronted by a tearful Eusébio. He pleaded for half an hour with Jimmy to at least come to his party. Finally, out of his respect and affection for Eusébio, Hagan agreed to go to the reception with Iris, but nothing would make him change his mind about leaving Benfica.

In due course, Hagan sued Benfica for a breach of contract but it took six years for his case to come to court. The judgment went in his favour and Benfica were ordered to pay compensation. However, Benfica appealed.

Hagan heard nothing more until about three years later when he received a letter out of the blue informing him that he had lost the appeal. Neither Hagan, nor his lawyers, knew that the appeal had been heard and they had been given no opportunity to attend. It seems that the powerful people running the club had called in a few favours, although Borges Coutinho himself had stood down as club president in 1976.

Even without the Eusébio testimonial incident, it is questionable how much longer Hagan would have remained as coach of Benfica, since a fourth season would have been almost unprecedented for the club. Five out of his six predecessors had lasted only one year (the sixth less than two years), and after his departure the next three coaches only lasted a year. It was a tribute to Hagan's ability and professionalism that he had served the club successfully for a little over three seasons. One can only wonder whether those Sheffield United directors who had said in 1957 that Hagan did not have the ability to be a coach ever saw the error of their ways.

Among the majority of Benfica fans Jimmy remained a legend and, for as long as he stayed in Portugal, he was treated as a hero. He could not walk down the street without being recognised and if he and Iris went out for a meal the owner of the restaurant would invariably refuse to charge them. This would annoy Hagan, who always believed in paying his dues, and he would insist that if he were not allowed to pay he would never eat in the restaurant again, much to the chagrin of the Portuguese, who simply couldn't understand his attitude.

Hagan was not the first, but was certainly one of the most successful British coaches in Portuguese football, paving the way for the likes of Malcolm Allison, Graeme Souness, John Mortimore and Bobby Robson in later years.

CHAPTER SIXTEEN

The End Game

After walking out of Benfica Hagan found himself at a loose end and he agreed to coach Estoril Praia for a few months. He received no money for this but since he was in the process of suing Benfica for compensation, perhaps he did not wish to muddy the waters. He did receive some benefits in kind, however. Estoril Praia were in the Third Division and, aided by Hagan's coaching, they won the League title. They followed this up by winning the Second Division in 1974/75, although by this time Hagan had moved on.

On 25 April 1974 Portugal was rocked by a revolution when the leader, Salazar, was toppled. This caused unease among many of the expatriates, some of whom left the country. Jimmy, too, was worried about his future, and that of his wife and family. He is on record as saying he would like to return to English football but presumably no offers were immediately forthcoming for he accepted a coaching contract with Al Arabi in Kuwait in 1974, a job that lasted for two years. Al Arabi had been a leading Kuwaiti club since its formation in 1960.

It was yet another fresh experience for Jimmy and Iris. The contract was very lucrative, which no doubt compensated for the very hot climate and cultural differences. It helped to have a number of old friends and colleagues also working in Kuwait at the time, including Billy Hodgson, a former Sheffield United teammate,

Graham Williams, the former West Bromwich Albion captain, and Peter McParland.

On one occasion when the club won a major tournament, a local sheikh invited all the players and management to his palace. The players were each given a house and car for their efforts, and Jimmy received an expensive canteen of cutlery, which he no doubt appreciated from his Sheffield connections.

In 1976 when his contract with Al Arabi ended, Jimmy and Iris were not thrilled at the prospect of returning to the UK and hunting for a job. Despite his clash with Benfica, the four years that they had spent in Portugal had been largely enjoyable. They had a number of friends there and Jimmy was still regarded as a top coach. So they returned to their 'second home' where Jimmy took a series of short coaching contracts with five different Portuguese clubs. This lasted until 1982, by which time he was sixty-four.

Jimmy's daughter, Jackie, had never left Portugal since she had a job working on an Anglo-Portuguese newspaper. She was surprised when she heard from the media that her father was back in Portugal, since he had not bothered to tell her!

The first contract was with Sporting Club of Portugal (Sporting Lisbon), which caused a sensation – and banner headlines in the newspapers – when it was announced, since Sporting are Benfica's biggest rivals. It was on a par with a Sheffield United manager accepting a job with Sheffield Wednesday – something that simply did not happen. But Hagan was his own man, and he owed Benfica no favours (the court case was still pending).

Some years later Manuel Fernandes recalled Hagan's arrival at the club:

I was playing my second season as a forward at Sporting when I was coached by Jimmy Hagan. I remember well the first training session. Do I remember! He put us through two and a half hours of hard, physical work and there were players who couldn't manage it and threw up! The training was intense. On match days, Hagan was not a great conversationalist and would tell us the line-up 1 to 11, saying only 'Play well'.

I remember an episode on the day of a Portuguese Cup tie: Mister Hagan had a 'thing' for walks. Before lunch he made us do a four-kilometre fast-paced walk. At that time, high-heeled shoes were in fashion for men. Nobody was warned, so half the group finished the walk with their shoes over their shoulders!

He was a great professional, rigorous but very human with a very special sense of humour. A true gentleman.

Jose Manuel Delgado, Sporting's goalkeeper, also had fond memories of the enigmatic Hagan:

He used to say, with wry humour, that he did not drink alcohol: 'I leave that to my wife who drinks for me and herself.'

He had many sayings (besides the famous 'no comment'), one of which was when the forwards were training. Each time they kicked a ball over the goal and into the stands he would say, with that English accent he never lost, 'Eusébio never scored a goal over the crossbar, always under it.' Another was, 'If you train for two hours every day, you'll be strong enough to run for ninety minutes on a Sunday.'

A hard worker, and stubborn, he forbade any vitamins or other supplements for his players, and strictly defended his rights as a coach. One day we had a dispute about the players' food and the following day Hagan brought his contract to show a clause under which he had final say in the players' diet.

Even so, Jimmy Hagan won the hearts of his players, earned their respect and was remembered with affection long after he had moved on. For example, who would imagine Hagan spending time in the sauna with his players telling them about his exploits in the Second World War? Or that, on match days, he would often turn up with soil under his fingernails and explain to us, in great detail, how he had been arranging his garden?

The contract with Sporting Lisbon lasted for just one season, and the club finished second, behind Benfica, in the First Division. Sporting also reached the semi-finals of the Portuguese Cup. Jimmy could feel satisfied with another job well done.

After a break, Jimmy agreed to coach Boavista for the 1978/79 season. In comparison with Benfica and Sporting, Boavista Futebol Clube, from the Boavista neighbourhood of Oporto, the Portuguese second city, was a relatively small outfit, having just been promoted to the First Division after many years in the lower leagues. Hagan enjoyed his time there and seemed more relaxed, with less pressure on him than at the big clubs. They finished ninth in the First Division that year, but sensationally won the Portuguese Cup. Remarkably, they had to play both the semi-final and final twice after objections from Sporting on a technicality, but Boavista still came out on top.

Throughout the final Hagan incongruously clutched a little blonde doll with a knitted bonnet and black and white dress − a lucky mascot in the team's colours that he had been given by a well-wisher. The mascot certainly seemed to work − with a little help from Hagan's own 'magic', of course!

The win meant a lot to Jimmy, and photographs after the presentation of the trophy show him ecstatic, and wreathed in smiles − with no sign of the famous poker face.

For the following season (1979/80), Jimmy changed clubs again and coached Vitória Futebol Clube, Setúbal. This proved something of a challenge for the club finished twelfth in the First Division. Setúbal is a small town to the south-east of Lisbon and its football club had been in existence since 1910.

It was all change again for the 1980/81 season when he coached Belenenses. Jimmy took them to the semi-final of the Portuguese Cup, where they were beaten by Benfica. Founded in 1919 and based in the Belém quarter of Lisbon, Belenenses is, like its neighbour Sporting Lisbon, a general sports club catering for a range of activities, although it is best known for its football team. Under Hagan that season they finished eleventh in the First Division.

Jimmy had one final contract as a coach when he looked after Estoril Praia again for the 1981/82 season. They finished twelfth in the First Division.

After finishing with professional football Jimmy had no intention of turning his back on the game that he loved, so he offered to coach a local expatriates' team, the Lisbon Casuals, on an informal, unpaid basis. After the pressures of top-level football management, Jimmy was able to relax and enjoy himself and he amazed the amateur footballers with his skill, even though he was now approaching the age when he could draw his pension!

Jimmy and Iris were popular figures at social functions during their years in Portugal. Jimmy was a stalwart member of the St George's Society and could always be counted on to help with community activities and the British Legion.

He was also a founding member of the Charity Bridge Association which was formed in November 1981. As the name suggests, any profits went to charity. Card games had interested Jimmy ever since his Army days, and footballers generally are inveterate card players, since it helps to pass the time on long journeys to away games.

Jimmy and Iris continued to enjoy life in sunny Portugal, living in Estoril, and they also kept in touch with a number of players that Jimmy had coached, especially Eusébio, who remained a close friend.

They did make occasional visits back to the UK, however, usually keeping a low profile. At family gatherings he would often be reluctant to talk about his football career. He was far more interested in reminiscing about the old days, his pigeons, whippets, and so on. A coach of some of Europe's finest football teams he may have been, but he never forgot his roots. Although a large section of the Sheffield public had adopted him as a 'favourite son' he always regarded himself primarily as a Geordie.

During a visit in August 1985 Jimmy was prevailed upon to appear on a BBC Radio Sheffield phone-in with the then sports editor, Robert Jackson, and to attend a social evening at Bramall Lane, where he answered questions from the floor and was greeted enthusiastically by many of the older fans.

One predictable question concerned the relative merits of Portuguese and English football (at a time when English players were often criticised for their lack of quality, compared to continental players). Hagan's reply was surprising: 'English football is more exciting and direct; Portuguese football is often boring.' Did this reveal some disillusionment with Portuguese football? Perhaps it showed some regrets that he had not been able to remain in English football longer, although Hagan's utterances did, at times, need to be taken with the proverbial pinch of salt.

Some of those who hung around to try to snatch a private word with their hero may have been a little disappointed. They found that Jimmy was happy to talk about football, but less keen to talk about himself. Most successful sports stars are only too happy to bask in their former glories and will discuss matches and events ad nauseam, but not Jimmy. Fans who accosted him with comments such as 'I saw you at Bramall Lane that day when you scored a hat-trick' or 'Do you remember that goal you scored against so and so?' would find that he would politely steer the conversation away from himself and probably ask them a question instead. He hated to be put on a pedestal.

However, he did enjoy seeing his old teammates, Alf Ringstead, Albert Cox and Fred Furniss. Together they replayed many games and all agreed that the best part of football is on the field, playing it.

During the same visit he was guest of honour at a Sheffield United match against Wimbledon and was introduced to the crowd on the pitch. Even though the majority of spectators were too young to have ever seen him play, his reputation at the club was still huge. He received a standing ovation that brought many of the older supporters – Jimmy's generation – close to tears, and must surely have affected the great man himself.

Jimmy's dry sense of humour, which had sometimes got him into trouble over the years, caused a bit of bother on this occasion. When

Jimmy saw the ground at Bramall Lane, with all the new stands and other improvements, he made an off-the-cuff comment: 'There was nothing like this when I was here. Mind you, they've paid for this with the money they didn't pay me.' This was reported in the local press by journalist Tony Pritchett and was mistaken as criticism of the club, Sheffield United.

Whilst there is little doubt that Jimmy did make a quip on these lines it was not intended for public consumption. He was probably making the point that if he had been playing in the days after the maximum wage was abolished he could have made a lot of money out of the game.

He was back in Portugal when he received cuttings of the newspaper articles. He took exception to the way his comment was presented, out of context, in the press and he wrote to the editor of the *Sheffield Telegraph*, pointing out that 'Sheffield United paid me all the money I was entitled to and also gave permission for a testimonial match to be played at Bramall Lane.' Certainly nobody at Sheffield United had taken offence over his reported comment and his image remained untarnished.

Despite the many knocks that Jimmy had received from football – particularly his lack of full England caps, and his abrupt departure from several of the clubs he managed – he was never bitter, and he often remained on good terms with people who had caused him grief in former times. He seemed able to put behind him decisions made for professional reasons, and maintain personal friendships regardless.

Jimmy and Iris celebrated their golden wedding anniversary in 1990, by which time Jimmy had turned seventy. Iris had stuck by him through all the ups and downs of his career, and put up with his moods and occasional bouts of temper. She was a feisty woman and could hold her own in an argument. On her part, Iris had been a heavy smoker all her life, something that Jimmy – who did not smoke at all – tolerated.

Around the time of the golden wedding anniversary, family and friends began to notice that Jimmy was becoming increasingly forgetful.

As the episodes became worse it was obvious that this was not just 'old age', but the early signs of Alzheimer's disease.

Jimmy and Iris returned permanently to England in 1993 and lived in Walsall where Iris took care of her ailing husband until she died suddenly of a stroke in 1996.

The family now decided to move Jimmy to a nursing home where he could receive the care and supervision that he needed, and chose Ascot Lodge, Intake, in Sheffield.

Jimmy survived to enjoy his eightieth birthday on 21st January 1998, but a few weeks later he suffered a stroke. He was transferred to Hallamshire Hospital where, after ten days, he died peacefully in the early hours of 27 February.

Obituaries appeared not only in the *Sheffield Star* and some national newspapers, but also in the north-east, where their Geordie legend had not been forgotten. The Portuguese papers also reported Jimmy's death extensively.

The funeral was held on 4 March 1998, at 2.30p.m., the service fittingly taking place at St Mary's Church, Bramall Lane – just yards from where he played much of his football with Sheffield United – followed by cremation at the City Road cemetery. Hundreds came to pay their respects, including former teammates and associates, and supporters of all ages, including some too young to have ever seen him play.

Tributes were many and varied. One lifelong fan of Hagan, Les Briddon, declared that he would run a lap of the Bramall Lane pitch every year on the anniversary of Hagan's death, and he has kept his word to this day.

Messages of condolence were received from everywhere, including some of Jimmy's old players in Portugal. The great Eusébio told a journalist in Portugal:

> I am in mourning. The death of Jimmy Hagan is another huge loss
> to football. He was a great man, both as a coach and in his private
> life and I can also say that he was a great friend of mine. With him

leading the team we won three titles and would have won a fourth but for some problems when he decided he ought to leave. It was a shame, but everyone has his own ways and he made the decision he thought best. That's how he was.

Hagan left an impression on Benfica and on me. Under him, I finished my career in midfield and scored 43 goals. It was my second 'Golden Boot'. Our friendship extended to our families and that is why I have already phoned his daughter in England to send my condolences. No-one is immortal, but I am sincerely very sad that Jimmy Hagan has died. That is why, in a tribute to him as a man and all he represented to me, I am today dressed in mourning.

Postscripts

TOMMY LAWTON'S VIEW OF HAGAN
FROM *FOOTBALL IS MY BUSINESS* — 1946

Quiet, thoughtful, it can be truly said of Jimmy, as I have often heard it expressed, that the spectators do not see half of the good work he does. Surely this is the secret of a successful schemer? Jimmy goes through his routine so unobtrusively, yet is the master craftsman. I have had many opportunities of studying him in play, not only in international and Army games, but during the two years we played alongside each other in the Aldershot side during the war. He once helped me score six goals for Aldershot… and every one was made in a different fashion!

FROM A FAN

Wonderful, Wonderful Jimmy Hagan
by Derek Hurst

Thou shalt not worship idols
The Bible's word makes me a pagan
How I fell in love with t'wizardry
Of our great Jimmy Hagan.

It seems like only yesterday
But it's years let's make it plain
Since he graced us with all his skills
At dear old Bramall Lane.

The Boards of then, no different
Just business, cash and scowls
Nearly did an horrendous deal
Of selling him to the Owls.

Odd ball players of today we have
Like Gazza filling bar tills
So what compared was Jimmy worth
With his dedication and his skills?

When poor old Jimmy left this earth
At his service in a shroud
He packed our St Mary's Church
He still could pull a crowd.

Though gone from us he's still there
Our thoughts of him you'll not sever
Whoever you're playing for up there
You're in our minds for ever.

So sorry God, tho' I worship thee
And the Book says I'm a pagan
Just do us a favour pal
Take care of our Jimmy Hagan.

MICHAEL PARKINSON

FROM *THE DAILY TELEGRAPH* — 28 DECEMBER 1998

You only had to see Jimmy Hagan walk on to the park to remember him. Like Len Shackleton, Raich Carter, Peter Doherty, Wilf Mannion and other great inside forwards (that's what they used to call them), he was the star.

They were the players who owned the park because they were the mastermind of their team. Before the game was played at the speed of light there was a time when certain footballers were allowed to dwell on the ball and dictate the ebb and flow of the game; players with a special talent for finding time where there was none. People paid to see them. My father didn't say. "I think we'll watch Sheffield United today." He would say to me: "Let's go and watch Jimmy Hagan." He played once for England which gives you some indication of the competition he faced in the Forties and Fifties. He was strong, authoritative and could make the ball sing and dance: a man of stern visage but merry feet.

He was a club man (remember them?) and arguably Sheffield United's most illustrious player. Joe Mercer was the best man at his wedding. Off and on the field Jimmy Hagan belonged to the best of company.

EUSÉBIO'S TRIBUTE

FROM A SHEFFIELD UNITED FC PRESS RELEASE — 19 JANUARY 2001

Portuguese soccer legend Eusébio arrived at the Lane today to unveil a bronze statue of the late Jimmy Hagan, his friend and former manager at Benfica.

Jimmy, who died three years ago and would have celebrated his eighty-third birthday this weekend, is widely recognised as the greatest Sheffield United player of all time.

And the city's most famous son later struck up a lifelong friendship with Eusébio after guiding Benfica to three successive championships at the start of the 1970s.

Speaking to the press at Bramall Lane ahead of tonight's dinner in Hagan's honour, Eusébio said:

Jimmy is still in my heart to this day and I can see exactly why he was so popular with the people of Sheffield.

He was my coach at Benfica between 1970 and 1973 and I remember him being a manager who knew how to handle players well.

He always offered me good advice and told me where I should be playing to get the best out of me.

He was also a strong disciplinarian and when he first arrived, we were surprised by the physical preparation for games.

It's a testimony to him that I am here today and it will be a very emotional moment when I unveil the statue. Jimmy deserves this recognition because he was a good player, a wonderful manager and a great man.

Other titles published by The History Press

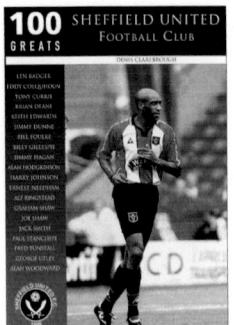

Sheffield United Football Club 100 Greats
DENIS CLAREBROUGH

Sheffield's 'golden years' of success began only nine years after their foundation in 1889. This book celebrates 100 of the club's greatest players, featuring biographies, statistics and an extensive selection of photographs, many of which have never been published before. This book will prove an enthralling read and a valuable reference work for supporters of all ages.

978 07524 2264 0

Voices of '66 Memories of England's World Cup
NORMAN SHIEL

Still remembered as England's final hour, this book captures the heady days when football actually came home. Including reminiscences from fans, players, administrators and television commentator Kenneth Wolstenholme, as well as many illustrations, this book will breathe life into a vital part of England's sporting heritage.

978 07524 3929 7

Ferenc Puskás Captain of Hungary
AN AUTOBIOGRAPHY

The captain of the great Hungary side that dominated world football in the 1950s, Ferenc Puskás was a charismatic and sublimely talented footballer who scored a phenomenal 83 goals in 84 international matches. With an incredible football brain and a left foot deadly in its power and accuracy, he was the key man in a footballing revolution that changed the game forever. This is his story.

978 07524 4435 2

Yorkshire County Cricket Club Classic Matches
MICK POPE AND PAUL DYSON

Relive the significant matches in the history of Yorkshire CCC, English cricket's most successful team in the County Championship. From the first match through to the most dramatic encounters of the twenty-first century, this volume recalls the thrills and spills of 50 memorable matches. Compiled by two of Yorkshire's most prominent cricket historians, the book features match reports, scorecards and many rare illustrations.

978 07524 3787 3

If you are interested in purchasing other books published by The History Press, or in case you have difficulty finding any of our books in your local bookshop, you can also place orders directly through the website
www.thehistorypress.co.uk